Thank for listening! !,

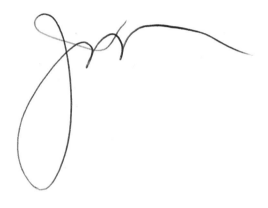

WHAT YOU DON'T KNOW ABOUT

LISTENING

COULD FILL A BOOK

Jon F. White
Alexandra Taketa

LEADERSHIP EDITION

Cover Design: Melissa Marie (www.TangerineMenagerie.com)
Interior Design: Wes Garlatz (www.StudioWes.com)

ISBN-13: 978-09915278-0-9
Printed in the United States of America
First Printing, May, 2014

Dedication

To Hope, Rick, Skylar, and Sierra for the way in which they listen to us.

CONTENTS

Acknowledgements

Our passion for writing this book about listening has met with tremendous support along the way.

Our greatest appreciation goes to our editor, Hope Sherwood of Artichoke Communications. We have tremendous respect for the way she transformed and elevated our sentences to make them more accessible to you, the reader, while retaining the full intent of our writing. Hope even conceived the title of this book...and we both love it!

Long before we set pen to paper, Jill Tomac helped us hone our point of view on communication skills while facilitating leadership programs. William Barton reminded us of the important part that listening plays in demonstrating emotional intelligence.

Terie Scerbo of Qualcomm, Inc. encouraged us to explore the willingness of an individual to seek feedback on their leadership. She also introduced us to the work of Dr. Daniel Wilson at the

Harvard Graduate School of Education. Terie's prodding resulted in an additional chapter that includes some note-worthy findings from Dr. Wilson's field studies on high-performing teams.

Stanlee Phelps, coauthor of *The Assertive Woman*, clarified the critical definition of "assertiveness" for us. She also introduced us to Bev Kaye, coauthor of *Love 'Em or Lose 'Em*. Bev became a great mentor and we are forever grateful to her for her insights, openness, boundless energy, and encouragement.

Will Sproule gave us copious notes on every chapter, helping us to improve the "feel" of the book. Rinny White tried out a number of the practice exercises and gave us useful feedback. Special thanks to Lori Mazan who, in the last hours, helped drag us to the finish line with her wisdom and sense of humor.

There are countless friends, family members, clients, and colleagues who deserve thanks as well. What we know about listening is a byproduct of all those interactions. Many of you gave us the energy to complete this two-year journey and we are grateful that we never traveled alone.

Part 1:
What You Need
to Know

1

Why You Need a Book on Listening

Isn't it interesting that you believe you are a good listener, yet you know hardly *ANYONE ELSE* who is?

That's the dilemma we faced when we began to write this book. **Most everyone *thinks* they are a good listener.** They probably can't picture themselves needing—or heaven forbid—***buying***, a self-help book on that subject.

But anyone who has experienced the results of poor listening can name an endless number of people who should read this book. Is one of them YOU? Well, even if it isn't, you might know someone whose performance is derailing them or their organization. Perhaps you should make them a gift of *What You Don't Know About Listening (Could Fill a Book)!*

The Root of the Problem

In our work as Executive Coaches, we frequently find ourselves diagnosing the key barriers that keep an individual from operating at peak potential. This diagnostic journey is similar to the physician who tries to determine the root problem causing a patient's skin rashes, joint pain, and headaches. There could be many different reasons for these conditions. Or, there might be just *one root* from which all this pain arises—like their poor diet—that is causing all the havoc.

Our experience has shown us that *poor listening* is a very common *root cause* of leadership "pain". It shows up as a factor in about one-third of the coaching we do.

Here are some symptoms to look for:

- **The Leader is perceived to be**
  - » someone who avoids delivering difficult messages
  - » an inadequate communicator
  - » arrogant, or always wanting to "do it their own way"

- **The Leader's team does not execute well**
- **The Organization is not selecting, retaining or developing top talent**
- **Motivation is low**
- **Counterproductive conflict exceeds cooperation, and finger-pointing is a common practice**
- **Customer satisfaction is low**

If you recognize (and are suffering from) any of these outcomes of inadequate listening skills, you are probably pretty interested in learning how to rectify things.

We're confident that, in the first few chapters of this book, we can teach you the concepts of how to **really listen**. Sooner than you'd think, you'll gain the tools to build more successful and productive relationships with your clients, colleagues, and employees. *But wait, there's more...*you'll find that these tools will come in handy in your personal relationships as well.

However, if you are only concerned about giving off the *perception* of listening and your primary motive is to better manipulate others, then this book may not be for you. Stop reading right now and pass this book on to someone else *who will probably become your boss in a year's time.*

On the other hand, if you want improve your relationship with your boss, a peer, or those who report to you—and truly recognize the opportunity that comes from understanding each of them better—please read on.

Helen Peters and Robert Kabacoff of The Management Research Group (MRG) published a paper in 2005 entitled, "Attributes of the Most Effective Leaders in the Technology Sector." They studied 1,412 highly educated leaders from 21 different organizations using an anonymous 360-degree feedback tool.

They found that to be considered a good *business manager,* a leader needs to:

- **Be strategic, which means to take a long-range, broad approach to problem solving and decision making through objective analysis, thinking ahead, and planning**

They also found, that to be considered a good people manager, a leader needs to:

- **Demonstrate an active concern for people and their work**
- **Value the ideas and opinions of others**
- **Have a more inclusive decision-making style**

Interestingly, their research showed a strong correlation between each of these behaviors and listening.

Listening is the skill that bridges your effectiveness as a leader of people with your success as a business leader.

How Do You Communicate?

Ah, but what often gets in the way of proper listening is an individual's personal *style of communication*. A large number of leaders fall into one of two categories:

Aggressive

These leaders **are comfortable being aggressive** when they need to get things done with their equally capable superiors, peers and subordinates. The aggressive leader is *less likely to be perceived as a listener*. They frequently use persuasion to get things done, which may lead to compliance rather than commitment. They are typically comfortable with, or unaware of, conflict.

Our approach is intended to provoke an aggressive leader to become more aware of their behavior and choose new skills that force them to listen.

Passive

These folks are **uncomfortable asserting themselves** with equally capable superiors, peers, and subordinates. They are probably pretty good listeners but they may be concerned that conflict will arise when they transition to expressing their expectations and concerns.

Our approach leverages skills that passive managers can, with practice, learn to assimilate comfortably into their leadership style. The result is a substantially more effective leader.

KEY THOUGHT
Instead of being either passive or aggressive, we encourage leaders to be assertive.

What Does it Mean to be Assertive?

There are still many misunderstandings about the true meaning of assertiveness. "Some think assertiveness is a just a milder, 'nicer' form of aggressiveness. Yet the two are entirely distinct sets of behaviors with different objectives and motivations."[1] Take a look at the definition of assertiveness.

> **Assertiveness:** *A form of communication in which needs or wishes are stated clearly with respect for oneself and the other person in the interaction.* **Assertive** *communication is distinguished from* **passive** *communication (in which needs or wishes go unstated) and* **aggressive** *communication (in which needs or wishes are stated in a hostile or demanding manner).*[2]

Our approach helps you evolve into a more collaborative, direct, and honest leader because it lays the groundwork for you to truly hear the other person—and for them to hear you.

A Book in Three Parts

In the coming chapters we'll ask you to explore new behaviors and practice new skills. In Parts I and II, we give you the core concepts that support what *listening really is*. You'll need each concept to build the strong foundation for your new behaviors. Whenever you need to, return to these early chapters and they will give you confidence.

---

1   Stanlee Phelps and Nancy Austin, *The Assertive Woman*, 4th Edition, Impact Publishing, 2002
2   Kristalyn Salters- Pedneault PhD, "What is assertiveness?," About.com, February 19, 2009

Insecurity comes from not understanding the concept. —Plato

You may quickly understand the concepts that are discussed in just the first few chapters, but employing a specific new behavior takes time and effort. You could feel awkward at first. Most all the chapters include **Skill-Building Exercises** that are designed to help you imprint and own each of these behaviors. *(I must admit that I myself don't usually do any practice exercises, but the ones we've included will really help to increase your confidence before you go "live" with a new behavior. —Jon)*

In Part III, we demonstrate how to use your new listening skills in all the common leadership situations you encounter on a daily basis.

What You Don't Know About Listening (Could Fill a Book) is intended to be a career-long reference handbook that will guide you through the communication potholes on the road to your ever-advancing career.

Keep in mind that you've been using your old listening skills all your life. Naturally, it will take time to assimilate these new behaviors into your everyday conversations. Be patient. Practice. Celebrate your successes. And above all, keep listening.

2

What Listening Is

Even if you were born with the ability to hear, you might not have acquired the ability to listen. Hearing is a physiological capability. Listening is a collection of learned behaviors supported by specific skills.

You learn the behaviors of listening first from your parents, then other family members, then friends, classmates and...well, you get the picture. One typically learns how to listen by first *observing, and then copying the behavior.* Unfortunately, you can pick up some bad habits in the process. That's because you are learning from people who don't know how to listen themselves!

Research shows that basic communication skills are developed by the age of 12. It isn't until our twenties, when our brains more fully develop, that we become aware of social nuances and the finer aspects of communication and listening.[1] Unfortunately by then, many of those bad habits learned in our early years have

---

1   Newberg and Waldman, *Words Can Change Your Brain*, 2012

already become ingrained. This book intends to teach you new skills and help you "unlearn" those entrenched habits so that you can become an expert listener.

Let's try a metaphor. Learning to listen is kind of like learning to swim. Most people learn to swim when they are young. But if you want to be a competitive swimmer, your swim coach will probably make you unlearn some bad habits you fell into at an early age and then replace them with more efficient skills. To really excel, you'll have to improve your stroke technique, build your strength and endurance, and then practice consistently. The same applies to listening skills. If you want to be an excellent listener, then it's out with the bad habits and in with the good ones. Oh, and by the way, you also have to practice.

KEY THOUGHT
Listening is a collection of learned behaviors supported by specific skills.

So Why Go to All of this Effort?

Most people want to be perceived as collaborative, empathetic, and consensual. That includes you, right? But to many, that perception seems to conflict with their desire to be direct, decisive, and assertive.

You need to balance these attributes if you wish to be regarded as a highly effective leader. There is one elegant solution to balancing all these perceptions. You guessed it—*listening!*

What Behaviors Support Listening?

Let's say you want to demonstrate to someone that you are listening to them. List below the behaviors you would display to assure them that you are paying rapt attention:

1._____

2._____

3._____

4._____

5. _____

Which **one** on your list would you guess has the greatest power to indicate that you are truly listening? **Note:** Select carefully, because this amazing listening tool is sure to lead others to think that you are strategic, empathetic, compassionate, and consensual.

Well, after querying thousands of people about this topic, we've found that a majority will choose *eye contact* as the most effective listening behavior. At our seminars, we perform an interesting experiment. We ask a participant to tell us about something they did yesterday, while we visibly demonstrate good eye contact for the entire audience.

Admittedly, our eye contact during this experiment is a bit piercing, but we want to be sure they can "see" us listening. They talk for a minute or so and then we ask them whether they were convinced that we were listening to them. Most say they were. (Others are just really weirded out by our stare!)

Then, we reveal to all that we did not, in fact, hear a word that they were saying. It's the truth! We were staring with our eyes—even occasionally nodding our head—and **not paying one bit of attention** to what was communicated.

Most everyone in the room readily admits that they themselves have been guilty of this same behavior.

Don't get us wrong—good eye contact should be a part of a sincere face-to-face conversation. However, we are so good at using eye contact to make someone believe we are listening to them, that we can actually fake it (and often get away with it)!

Say your friend begins to tell you about their weekend at the beach. Immediately, your mind begins to shift to your own agenda. You consciously engage in eye contact, and even throw in a few vocal affirmations to assure your friend that you are listening. But what's actually going on in your mind while you *look like* you're listening? What is it that most of us are doing while our body language and vocal affirmations attempt to convince otherwise?

Bingo! We are busy forming the next statement we want to make as soon as we can get a word in.

When your friend mentioned their trip to the beach, your mind suddenly started to generate all the things **YOU** want to say about the beach. "I went to the beach, too," or "I always get sunburned when I go," or "My kids are always nagging me to go." You get the picture.

Talking About Ourselves Feels Good

Sounds like we are pretty egocentric, doesn't it? Well, science would agree that *we are*. Research confirms that, "talking about ourselves triggers the same sensation of pleasure in the brain as food or money."[2] That means that the barriers to paying attention to another human are more than simply the distractions in the room…they may stem from the chemicals in our brain!

---

2   Tamir and Mitchel, *Proceedings of the National Academy of Sciences.*

"We love it when people listen to us. Why else would we tweet?" —Robert Lee Hotz, *"Science Reveals Why We Brag So Much,"* The Wall Street Journal, May 8, 2012

Another barrier to paying attention as we listen is our natural tendency to be critical of what's being said. According to Rogers and Roethlisberger,[3] "One major obstacle to communication is people's tendency to evaluate. We all have a natural urge to judge, evaluate, and approve (or disapprove) another person's statement." Our tendency to evaluate shuts down the listening process and could well stir up defensiveness in the other person.

What that means is that, while someone else is speaking, we are already planning our response AND that response could very likely sound like a criticism. Don't beat yourself up. Remember, these are behaviors you probably learned by the time you were 12 years old.

Earlier in this chapter, we asked you to think about the behaviors that you use to give someone the perception that you are listening to them.

Your list likely included:

- **Eye contact**
- **Positive body language**
- **Vocal affirmations ("yes", "uh-huh", etc.)**
- **Paraphrasing**
- **Asking questions**

---

3 *"HBR Classic"*, November 1991

We think that all of these behaviors help reinforce that we are listening, but as you yourself know, eye contact can mask the fact that you are not truly listening. Body language and vocal affirmations can be "faked" as well.

If someone is recounting a story and you attentively face them, make eye contact, and vocalize occasional sounds of approval, they may feel they are being heard. However, they too have previously used these behaviors while pretending to listen and they know that you could possibly be simulating attentiveness. Consequently, there is no way for them to be sure that you truly got the message.

How to Prove You are Listening

Asking a question is the best way to indicate that you are truly listening. And we maintain that asking "that next great question" is an elegant solution for improving your communication skills— elegant, because it is marked by appropriateness and simplicity. And yes, it's a simple solution, but that doesn't make it easy. That's why *What You Don't Know About Listening (Could Fill a Book)* does in fact fill a book!

KEY THOUGHT
Asking a question is the best way to indicate that you are truly listening.

As it turns out, asking a question may actually force you to listen. We say "may", because it has to be the *right question*. Before we describe the attributes of the right question, let's spend a bit more time on exactly what it is about a question that convinces someone that you are actually listening.

If you follow someone's statement with a question, you are consciously and subliminally indicating that you want to hear more. Your request for additional information about something *specific* will demonstrate that you were listening.

This specific question also has the potential to show that we care about what the person had to say, which starts us down the path of being perceived as **empathetic**.

So why would you care about being perceived as empathetic? Well, we believe it's important for highly effective leaders to show this kind of support when interacting with people. Let's take a look at what empathy is exactly. We like the definition that Management Research Group (MRG) uses.

Empathy: *Demonstrating an active concern for people and their needs.*

And the best way to show "an active concern for people and their needs" is to listen to them—*by asking questions*. You're bound to get into trouble if you assume (without asking) that you know what their concerns are.

A specific question also has the power to show that you are able to be **consensual**. If, when having a business discussion with a peer, you hear them express an idea about a project, but you follow their idea with an idea of your own, they may not think you are listening. But if you follow their thought with a specific question about what they said, they'll feel assured that you listened to them. This raises the potential that they will perceive you as being **consensual**. And that's a good thing, right?

Probably, depending on your definition of consensual. In our work, we hear that word thrown around so often that there's no consensus about what the word consensual means! Let's turn to MRG again for a good definition.

> **Consensual:** *Valuing the ideas and opinions of others and collecting their input as part of your decision-making process.*

The process of "collecting input" requires you to listen. It doesn't necessarily mean you must agree or compromise. Might it take more time at first? Yes, but with practice, your ability to ask the right questions will improve. And with the addition of selected inputs, so will the quality of your decisions.

Chapter Summary

- Listening is a cluster of behaviors.

- Many of those behaviors can be faked. *(Obviously, we don't recommend this!)*

- Asking a question is the best way to demonstrate that you are listening.

- Demonstrating that you are listening enhances the perception that you are strategic, empathetic, and consensual.

In the next three chapters, we will describe the characteristics of a great question and give you a chance to practice some skills.

But before we start changing those behaviors, discover what kind of listener you are today by doing the following exercises.

SKILL-BUILDING EXERCISES

Be Honest. How Good a Listener are You Really?

Give yourself a moment to stop and think. Write down your thoughts. This space is for you - we encourage you to be open and honest. No one is looking over your shoulder. The only one who benefits from your candor and your work here is you.

1. What have you been doing when it comes to listening? What do you currently do to show that you are listening? What specific behaviors or actions have you been using to demonstrate that you are listening?

   _____

   _____

   _____

   _____

2. What does listening mean to you?

   _____

   _____

   _____

3. How do you feel when someone really listens to you? *(Think about a specific situation or instance in which someone truly listened to you. What did you think? What were the emotions and feelings that were evoked? What was the impact on you?)*

   _____

   _____

   _____

4. How do you feel when you truly listen to someone else?

_____

_____

_____

5. What would becoming a better listener do for you?

_____

_____

_____

6. What do you have to gain from listening more effectively in your work and home life?

_____

_____

_____

7. In what area do you need to focus more energy on listening?
    a. With someone specific?
    b. About a specific topic / strategy / project?
    c. Within a particular area of your business?

8. If you truly listened to the ideas of your team, colleagues, employees, or clients, about _____, what might they say?

a. Pick a "hot topic" for you and fill in the blank with that topic as you answer the question. You may need to answer this question for more than one "hot topic"— don't limit yourself.

_____

_____

_____

_____

_____

_____

_____

9. What would being a better listener bring to your leadership?

_____

_____

_____

_____

_____

_____

_____

10. What do you want to know more about that you don't know today?

_____

_____

_____

_____

_____

11. What would being a better listener bring to your relationships at work?

_____

_____

_____

_____

_____

We were given two ears and one mouth, so we ought to listen twice as much as we speak. —Ancient Proverb

3

Open-Ended Questions

An open-ended question is one that cannot be answered with a simple "yes" or "no". Potentially, the response could uncover great insights into the other person's thoughts.

On the other hand, a closed-ended question begs a simple "yes" or "no" answer. We can expect to learn very little about what the other person is really thinking or feeling.

When you ask someone an open-ended question, you invite them to tell you more. It suggests to them that you are so interested, you want to go deeper. What's more, it demonstrates that you didn't just listen—you actually *heard* them. Using an open-ended question is a great way to show someone that you value their ideas and—even more powerful—that you value *them*.

KEY THOUGHT
Ask open-ended questions when:
1. You want to know what someone is really thinking
2. You want someone to know that you are interested in what they have to say

A Story from Jon

I was running a medical device company that maintained two separate manufacturing locations. It was decided that, to become more efficient, we would close one facility and merge all manufacturing into one site. Unfortunately, only a few employees would be offered relocation. This was tricky because several of the employees who were not being offered relocation were key to making the move successful. Talking to those who would eventually be without a job would be a difficult conversation.

All managers struggle with how to start a difficult conversation. Admit it—you tend to procrastinate, and if you can, avoid it all together. After all, your employee is likely to become upset and could even direct all that anger at YOU!

That said, from a business standpoint, you need to know what the employee is actually thinking. This knowledge could affect your plans. And, from a compassionate standpoint, the employee may need your support to navigate the change that is coming their way. So, it's clear you must be properly prepared to conduct this conversation.

Now, Back to Jon's story...

After we announced the decision, I quickly arranged to talk with each of these key employees to determine if they would stay on through the move. One of the first employees I met with was Jim, the second-shift supervisor of the injection molding plant. If I wanted to be a coward and keep the meeting mercifully short, I could merely have asked a closed-ended question.

Here's what that might have sounded like:

Jon: "Are you okay?"   *(That's a pretty common approach.)*

Jim: "Yep."   *(A pretty common answer, even when's it's not true.)*

Jon: "Good."   *(End of conversation.)*

Or it could have sounded like this:

Jon: "Are you okay?"   *(Hey, I'm a slow learner!!)*

Jim: "Nope."   *(A pretty common—and terrifying—answer.)*

Jon: *(choose one of the options below...)*

- "Well, things will get better."
- "You'll be OK."
- "I'll check back with you in a few days."
- "Let me explain again why we had to do this."

In either scenario, Jon's not going to learn much from Jim's response. When you ask a closed-ended question, you usually have to add your own interpretation to the response you receive.

It's evident that in the example where Jim said he was okay, Jon didn't learn what Jim was *really* thinking.

And in the example where Jim said he *wasn't* okay, Jon would have to *assume* he knew Jim's thoughts. Then Jon would use that assumption to make a *persuasive* statement in the hopes that it resolved Jim's concerns. But persuasion can't help Jon learn anything—it can only inform Jim of *Jon's* point of view. It doesn't surface Jim's issues or generate his ideas on how to overcome those issues. And it definitely doesn't increase Jim's commitment to the change.

You'll find that an open-ended question is invaluable if you want to gather more information about what someone is *really* thinking or feeling.

Here's how Jon's actual conversation with Jim really went:

Jon: "What are your thoughts about yesterday's announcement?"

Jim: *"Well, my wife and I have been thinking about moving back to Minnesota. I guess this helps us make that decision."*

> *Okay, I know, you think I got off easy because in this case I wasn't confronted with anger. I promise you, there were many other conversations that weren't quite so painless. The important thing about this conversation is that I learned something valuable from asking an open-ended question. I learned that Jim had a plan. He and his wife were not in denial about the company's decision and they weren't resenting the fact that they were not included in the relocation group.*

Asking an open-ended question is the first step on the path to becoming a better listener because it opens up the doorway of conversation.

Are there times when it's better to ask a closed-ended question? Yes. Like when it's an emergency. *(Is this the right fire extinguisher?)* Or when you need to get that person who is famous for drifting off topic back to the task at hand. *(May we return to talking about why you postponed that important meeting?)*

Asking an open-ended question is the first step on the path to becoming a better listener because it opens up the doorway of conversation. From that opening, there is no limit to what you may discover.

Notice the difference between these closed and open-ended questions:

CLOSED-ENDED	OPEN-ENDED
Is this an effective strategy for you?	What makes this an effective strategy for you?
Is there more to be learned here?	What would double your learning in this experience?
It sounds like you have two choices—is that true?	What is another choice you could make besides the two in front of you?
It sounds like you have explored all the options available—is that true?	What options might still be open to exploration?
Are you excited about your new role?	What is exciting to you about your new role?
Are you ready?	What do you need to do to prepare for this opportunity?

Chapter Summary

Ask Open-Ended Questions:

- To find out what someone is thinking.

- To show someone that you are interested in what they have to say.

SKILL-BUILDING EXERCISES

Developing our Listening Muscles

Some people are truly gifted and talented listeners. They intuitively know how to listen with masterful grace. Before you count yourself in that category, we would argue that those folks are few and far between. Most of us have room to improve. The good news is that because listening is a **behavior**, we can train and develop the **skills** that support it, just like we can develop a muscle—by exercising it! So let's begin.

1. **Closed vs. Open.** The goal of this exercise is to practice taking a closed "yes or no" question and translating it to an open-ended question. Try these:

   - So you didn't like that, huh?

   - Did you agree with the announcement?

   - Did you finish that project yet?

   - Did you lose the customer?

   - Shall we move ahead as planned?

   _____

   _____

   _____

   _____

   _____

See the next page for some suggestions.

2. Here are some possible ways to "open up" those questions:

CLOSED-ENDED	OPEN-ENDED
So you didn't like that, huh?	What did you think/feel about that experience?
Did you agree with the announcement?	What are your thoughts about the announcement?
Did you finish that project yet?	What can you tell me about progress on that project?
Did you lose the customer?	What is our relationship with this customer?
Shall we move ahead as planned?	What, if anything, do we need to consider before we move ahead?

3. **Practice Asking Open-Ended Questions.** The goal of this exercise is to start building your listening muscles by practicing asking open-ended questions. Ask a colleague or a friend to play a quick game with you for about ten minutes. Ask your partner to tell you about a favorite book, movie, or television program. See how many questions you can ask that are open-ended. Get curious and stay focused on their responses—this will help you generate more good open-ended questions.

4. **Ask Yourself Powerful Questions.** The goal of this exercise is to apply the practice of asking open-ended questions to a current work challenge that you're experiencing. What questions do

you need to ask yourself right now to help move forward in this area, relationship or challenging situation? Don't let yourself off the hook. Imagine which questions a great coach might ask you? Take some time to write down these questions and then answer them!

4

Vertical Questions

You've now learned that an open-ended question demonstrates that you are truly listening. Let's take this to the next level.

A **Vertical Question** is based on something the other person has just said. Asking open-ended questions that are vertical will force you to be more curious, making your questions more powerful. Let's imagine that you are asking someone about their recent vacation. If you don't employ vertical questioning, your conversation could sound like this:

You: "What did you do on your vacation?"

Them: *"We went snorkeling."*

You: "Where'd ya go?"

Them: *"We went to Bermuda."*

You: "Oh, we love Bermuda. Went there last year. Did you see the blah-blah-blah...?"

Did you notice how this typical conversation quickly turned to you adding your own perspective? You stopped listening and required them to start listening to YOU! This is a perfect example of how small talk is conducted.

Is there anything wrong with this? No. But it doesn't serve to demonstrate that you are truly listening. To them, it feels like you're not sincerely interested in what they have to say. If you use the listening technique illustrated above, you won't cement the perception that you are genuinely focused on their thoughts or feelings. Maybe that's okay.

If, however, you want to be perceived as a good listener, a great conversationalist, and a good friend, your chat might sound more like this:

You: "What did you do on vacation?"

Them: *"We went snorkeling."*

You: "Really? Tell me, what do you like about snorkeling?"

Them: *"It's just so relaxing."*

You: "What do you find relaxing about it?"

It's hard to say where a conversation like this might go because it rises above small talk. You are *forced to listen* so that you can formulate the next great question. Going vertical with your questions will help move you into a level of clarification, creativity, and collaboration. That would never be possible if you stayed at the surface and focused on your own opinions and experiences.

Some vertical questions are better than others. When we work with participants in our seminars, we find they usually ask weak questions that are activity-based.

You: "Where did you go?"

Them: *"Bermuda."*

You: "What did you see?"

Them: *"Fish."*

You: "What kind?"

Them: *"Yellow, blue, green..."*

Small answers equal small talk. Activity-based questions are fine for small talk. But successful vertical questions allow us to really get to know a person better because they are more focused on the person than a thing or activity. This tool helps you to discover how that person really thinks, what they value, and who they are.

Since the source of a good vertical question is derived from what the other person has just said, you are obligated to pay attention. And you are forced to pause and think about the next, best question to ask. What is going to be the right "thread to pull"?

Don't be afraid of taking a moment to think. Science confirms that a bit of silence is golden. A pause increases comprehension and connection by allowing both your brain and their brain to process thoughts more fully.[1] We'll talk more about the importance of pausing in Chapter 7, "Push Pause To Listen."

Let's get back to vertical questions. The source of a vertical question should not stem from any agenda you may have. You must suspend all agendas for the moment—except to *listen* to this other person so that they feel truly listened to.

---

1   MacGregor L. J., Corley M, Donaldson D. I., "Listening to the sounds of silence: Disfluent silent pauses in speech have consequences for listeners," *Neuropsychologia*, December 2010, 48 (14): 3982-92. Epub October 13, 2010.

The results for those we've taught to do this have been extremely positive. But there have been some doubters with concerns like these:

Doubter: *"This feels very unnatural."*

Us: Of course it feels unnatural. This is a new skill. We suspect you were uncomfortable the first time you tried to ride a bike. If you plan to try hang gliding, we're betting you'll be a bit uncomfortable doing that at first, too!

Doubter: *"The people I talk to will think this is strange behavior."*

Us: You'll probably be more conscious of this than they will be. That said, if you have not been a good listener in the past, showing up today with a new behavior may get some attention. We recommend making this change transparent. In other words, as you practice this behavior, tell your friend or coworker that you are trying something new.

Doubter: *"I feel like I'm getting too personal and people will be uncomfortable."*

Us: Not really. YOU are the uncomfortable one. THEY are being listened to, and let's face it—people like to talk about themselves. Vertical questions encourage that. Don't worry, it will get easier.

Doubter: *When you say we should ask Vertical Questions, don't you really mean Probing Questions?*

Us: Well, a probing question implies that the questioner has an agenda. It's the kind of driving query that TV's Perry Mason would ask during a courtroom cross-examination in order to win his argument. A vertical question is meant to gather information that enables you to progress towards a collaborative solution. Our intention isn't to put someone on the defense; we just want to foster mutual cooperation.

Are there times when you need to ask probing questions? Do you sometimes need to be more dominant than collaborative? Yes. But take our word for it; you probably *overuse* those skills and behaviors. Chances are you *underuse* the valuable vertical question.

KEY THOUGHT

Asking open-ended questions demonstrates that you are listening.

When you ask open-ended questions that are vertical, it will force you to be more curious, making your questions even more powerful.

With practice you'll learn when to stop going vertical in your conversations and move on to another "thread" or to another topic altogether. Often the listener will signal that you've gone deep enough.

They may:

- **Stop making eye contact**
- **Start shifting their posture**
- **Change the subject**
- **Break out in a cold sweat and tug at their collar** (Okay, that's a bit too deep.)

The situation will determine whether you respect that boundary. Of course, your casual conversations would come to a close. However, the manager of a critical project may have to weigh several factors before allowing a direct report to discourage a thorough conversation.

It Becomes Second-Nature

Great conversationalists who have mastered the skill of asking vertical questions can get to the point where the next vertical question becomes almost instinctive. The right questions seem to pop out of the information they are hearing, taking the dialog to a new and richer level of understanding.

It's important that your questions do, in fact, "pop" out of the information that the other person is sharing. If you use questions to *lead* the conversation rather than *respond* to the information, you'll sound just like our friend Perry Mason as he pummels the witness into confessing. Asking leading questions may be seen as working your own agenda, which could dampen understanding and undermine trust.

If you find yourself thinking about the next brilliant comment you're about to say, it's probably a clue that you're not going vertical. Stop, and ask an open-ended, vertical question.

The process of asking truly vertical questions helps you move away from your agenda because you are focusing on what the other person is saying, not what your own next move will be. When going vertical, you should feel unattached to yourself, your opinions, or your agenda. If you find yourself thinking about the next brilliant comment you're about to say, it's probably a clue that you're not going vertical—you are firmly inside your own experience.

There is a time and a place to share your own experience, to offer advice, and to provide counsel—but this isn't it. We'll get to practice that skill later. Right now we want to begin to open up the conversation. This requires that you set aside your own agenda, focus on what the other person is telling you, and become receptive to discovery.

Chapter Summary

- Ask vertical questions to show you are truly interested.

- Vertical questions will force you to be curious.

- With practice, vertical questions will seem to "pop" out of what the other person is saying.

SKILL-BUILDING EXERCISES

1. **Surface vs. Vertical.** The goal of this exercise is to understand the power of listening at a surface or activity-based level versus a personal level. During this exercise, your goal is to focus entirely on your own thoughts, experiences and opinions without going deeper into what the other person is saying. To do this exercise effectively, you'll need to ask a friend or colleague to take ten minutes to play this listening game with you.

   Round 1: Stay at the surface. Ask your partner to describe a recent vacation they took, including things that went well, what they enjoyed or didn't enjoy, and what activities they did on vacation. As your partner tells their story, your job is to listen to the story and interpret it entirely in terms of your own experience. Comment frequently to your partner about your own experiences, thoughts and opinions. While your partner talks, think about the following:

- How would you do this trip the same or differently?

- What does this story remind you of in your own life?

- What advice do you have for your partner?

- Do you have a similar story you could share from your own experience?

- How could you improve their story?

For example, if your partner tells you about their beach vacation, you might comment on how you dislike the beach, or talk about your own last trip to the beach, or even why they should have gone to the mountains instead of the beach.

Debrief: After about three minutes, stop and discuss what it was like for you to listen at a surface level and what it was like for your partner, who was being listened to at a surface level.

_____

_____

_____

_____

Round 2: Ask the same partner to share again the identical story. This time, be genuinely curious, asking open-ended and vertical questions. Remember to remain "neutral" and without an agenda while you are digging deeper into what the person says. Stay completely focused on what was just said, and allow that to be the source of your questions. Also, pay attention to your partner's values as they are expressed in the story. What do you learn about what they value and find important?

Debrief:

- Discuss what it was like to listen and be listened to beyond a surface level.

- What about this experience was different from Round 1 of this exercise?

- Which experience was more rewarding and enjoyable?

- What did you gain from this exercise?

_____

_____

_____

_____

_____

2. **Go Vertical.** The purpose of this exercise is to practice asking vertical questions and stretching beyond your current comfort zone. Focus on going deeper into one topic before switching to the next one. For example, ask a colleague, a friend or a family member to tell you about the town they grew up in as a kid. Do your best to ask as many vertical questions as you can about that topic before allowing the conversation to move on or come to a conclusion. After the conversation, reflect on the following:

- What did you find easy about coming up with vertical questions? What was challenging?

- How many layers "deep" were you able to go—five questions deep, or could you go even more?

- What did the experience feel like for you, the listener, and for the individual being listened to?

- What did you discover that you didn't know before?

_____

_____

_____

3. **Take a Field Trip.** The purpose of this exercise is to observe how typical conversations flow. Spend half an hour at a coffee shop (or any other busy venue) and just observe what is going on in the conversations around you. What do you notice about the "typical" conversation? What level of listening are most people exhibiting? How many layers "deep" does the typical conversation go?

_____

_____

_____

4. **Self-Evaluation.** The purpose of this exercise is to think about your own relationships (work, home, friendships, etc.). Where would you most benefit from practicing more deep listening? What do you need to do to begin using more open-ended and vertical questions?

_____

_____

_____

5

"What" Questions

We have been encouraging you to use questions to improve your relationships. But there is *one word* **that is commonly used to begin a question that could engender an uncomfortable response.** Use this word and watch the adrenaline course through your listener's veins.

That word is **"Why."**

How did this happen? How was this neuro-linguistic connection made? Well, when you were a child, your parents (probably rightfully) scolded you for many things. Perhaps you knocked over an expensive lamp while playing with your toys. Your parents pointedly asked you, "WHY were you playing with a ball in the living room?"

Then at school, your teacher reprimanded, "WHY didn't you do your homework?"

Now, you are fully grown, but how do you feel when your boss asks, "WHY is that report I've been asking you for still incomplete?"

KEY THOUGHT

Over time, you have been programmed to understand that a "why" question could suggest that you are somehow wrong. Worse yet, that question might be followed by a reprimand.

In your past, "Why" questions may have challenged your authority, honesty, or even the right to your own emotions.

It seems that humans around the world are encoded to react this way. We asked leaders who come from non-English speaking backgrounds to recall their own childhood mishaps. After translating our "why" question into their native tongue, a majority of those we interviewed immediately relived those childhood feelings of being scolded or shamed.

Imagine someone asking you this question and see if you—like most of us from any culture—are victim to this global programming.

English	**Why did you do that?**
Spanish	**¿Por qué hiciste eso?**
Mandarin	**你为什么这样做呢?**
Farsi	**چرا این کار را کردی؟**
German	**Warum hast du das getan?**
Vietnamese	**Tại sao bạn làm điều đó?**

A Magic Word

Interestingly, the word "What" normally lacks the judgment associated with the word "why". We've found that **beginning your question with "What" may help the conversation *feel* better for**

everyone involved. The value of the "What" question is strives to position you as a harmless questioner with a cu frame of mind. Disarming, no?

We discovered this in our own work with clients. When our questions began with "What", it invited them to uncover their own solutions. This process helped the client to analyze the problem, identify their own next steps, or even recognize their own limits and the need to ask for help from an expert.

Not only does this method develop one's capacity to problem solve, it's a key ingredient in increasing productivity, employee commitment, and in growing talent. Another bonus is that, as you ask more unbiased "what" questions (and get more curious), you are modeling the method for that individual to do this for themselves.

If you begin a question with "What" and then you genuinely become curious, you won't try to impose your will or way of thinking on the other person. Instead, you will:

- **Focus on *them*—not your own agenda—opening up a wider range of things for them to consider.**

- **Shed the role of expert, joining your conversation partner as an equal. That increases the likelihood that you'll collaborate to discover a mutually acceptable solution.**

We recommend you also use conditional language to signal to others that you are open to considering their opinion. Dr. Daniel Wilson, Harvard Graduate School of Education and Director of Harvard's Project Zero, observed this in how team members represent their knowledge with one another. *"In high-performing teams, members use conditional language ("it might be" or "it may be," etc.) about 70% of the time. They use assertive language ("it is" or "we are") about 30% of the time. But in low-performing teams it is almost the exact opposite: 70% assertive language and 30% conditional language."*

Imagine combining the power of "what" with the use of conditional language. It sounds like this—"**What might** the solution be?" rather than "**Here is** my solution."

So now you understand why we suggest you begin every question that you can with the word "What." And when you can start to sprinkle in some conditional language, you'll have the recipe for successful listening.

Other Behaviors Can Create a Barrier to Communication

Unfortunately, there isn't a "silver bullet" that can overcome every impediment to a verbal exchange. We can't promise that the word "What" will work every time. Asking good questions will increase your percentage of successful conversations; however you can unwittingly diminish those percentages. One good way to do that is using the wrong **tone of voice**.

Think about it…even dogs can distinguish between different tones of voice when hearing a command or an accusatory question. (***"WHAT-DID-YOU-DO?"***) Our spouses, kids, and coworkers are no different—they all hear the differences in your tone of voice.[1]

Imagine raising the volume and pitch of your voice as you say, "What the heck were you thinking?" Great, you used the word "What" but you will torch this chapter single-handedly with your fiery tone!

---

1   Andrew Newberg, M.D. and Mark Robert Waldman, *Words Can Change Your Brain: 12 Conversation Strategies to Build Trust, Resolve Conflict, and Increase Intimacy.* Hudson Street Press: 2012. Print.

Bottom line—make sure you use unbiased "What" questions to stay curious and neutral, share your thoughts in a conditional way, and try not to be tone deaf so you don't undo your good work!

Take a look at the examples below to get a feel for how the potential success of a conversation could change simply by choosing the unbiased over the judgmental question.

BIASED & JUDGMENTAL	UNBIASED
Why are you always so difficult to work with?	What do you need from me in order for us to work together effectively on this project? What would it look like for us to work well together?
Why did you make that decision?	What was the rationale behind your decision-making process?
Why did you include her on your team?	What talents does she bring to your team?
Why did you say yes?	What were your options? What outcome did you expect?
How could you have done this to us?	What is the impact of your decision?
Why were you so stupid?	What do you have to learn from this experience? What could you do differently next time?

Chapter Summary

- The word "why" can cause people to become defensive.

- Whenever possible, begin a question with the word "What."

- Remember that tone of voice and body language can also cause someone to become defensive.

SKILL-BUILDING EXERCISES

1. **Staying "Neutral".** The goal of this exercise is to become comfortable using "What" questions to help eliminate a defensive response. What problems can you imagine arising from the following "why" questions?

   - Why did you do that?

   - Why didn't you get it right?

   - Why do we have to invite Susie to the meeting?

   - Why did you decide to give Joseph a 10% raise?

   - Why didn't you tell me about this sooner?

   Now, try converting them into unbiased "What" questions.

   (See our suggestions on the next page.)

   _____

   _____

   _____

   _____

   _____

DEFENSIVE - "WHY" QUESTIONS	NEUTRAL - "WHAT" QUESTIONS
Why did you do that?	What was the benefit of doing it that way?
	What made that the best decision?
	What are the alternatives for how we could tackle this problem in the future?
Why didn't you get it right?	What information or support do you need?
	What do you need to move forward on the right track?
	What is holding you back from asking for help?
Why do we have to invite Susie to the meeting?	What value will Susie add to the conversation?
Why did you decide to give Joseph a 10% raise?	What were the criteria you used to determine Joseph's raise percentage?
	What were the criteria you used to determine who should be given a raise on your team?
Why didn't you tell me about this sooner?	What do we need to do now, given where we are in the process?

2. **The Impact of "What" Questions.** The goal of this exercise is to understand how "What" questions can impact the result of the

conversation. Ask a willing partner to play a game with you for about ten minutes.

Your job is to practice asking questions that start with the word "What." Pretend you are at a dinner party and sitting next to someone you don't know. Be curious—drop any external agenda you may have. Your goal is to have a "real" conversation with your partner.

Ask "What" questions about:

- Their life, work, and interests
- What makes them tick
- What they like and dislike
- What makes them unique
- What they value
- What aspirations they may have, etc.

Keep it real, stay curious, and use "What" questions as much as possible.

Debrief:

- What did this conversation feel like for the person being listened to and the person listening? How might it have felt if your questions instead began with the word "why?"
- Describe the tone of the conversation.
- What was the level of openness in the conversation for the person being listened to?
- What words would the person being listened to use to describe the conversation?
- What did you do well and what still needs practice? *(Remember to ask your partner for their candid feedback.)*

_____

_____

_____

_____

_____

Note: *Our experience tells us that the person being listened to will comment on feeling flattered and open to sharing willingly if the person asking the questions is authentically asking "What" questions from a place of curiosity. If this wasn't your result, please examine what you are doing to change the dynamic of the conversation.*

For example, imagine how different this conversation could feel if you pretended you were a lawyer cross-examining someone on the witness stand. Remember those "probing" questions we described earlier when we talked about the importance of asking vertical questions? Your partner would likely feel interrogated and therefore not open to sharing. Using "What" questions helps to disarm your partner. Remember to pay attention to tone, body language, your pace, and word choices in order to create an environment that is conducive to a productive and authentic dialogue.

3. **Get Curious.** The goal of this exercise is to practice being curious. Go to a busy venue (like a coffee shop or even your work cafeteria) and observe the folks around you. Without actually talking to anyone, let your imagination go...get curious as you think about each of the individuals you see.

   Write down a list of all the things about which you may be interested. For example:

- What makes them successful in their work?

- What talents do they contribute to work?

- What professional dreams do they have?

- What does their ideal work day look like?

- What do they enjoy about working with others?

- What are they really good at?

- What are the habits that help them be productive?

- What's important to them?

- What do they enjoy most about their work?

- What do they wish their boss would help them with at work?

_____

_____

_____

Now, if you are really brave, strike up a conversation with someone you don't know and do your best to be curious by asking "What" questions. If you don't feel brave enough to approach someone you don't know, try this exercise with someone you know well and trust. Fill them in on what you are up to and make sure they are willing to go along.

After the conversation, reflect on how this person responded to your "curious" approach. What did you learn? What was easy about this? What was challenging? Could you imagine bringing this method of asking "what" questions into your life (at work, home, and with friends)?

6

Putting Together a Great Question

The centerpiece of our listening approach is to ask questions that are open-ended, vertical, and begin with the word "What." Master this and you will be a remarkably better conversationalist, leader, and coach. The improvement can start as soon as tomorrow.

Compare these two conversations between a leader and an important direct report:

Conversation Number 1

Leader: Any concerns about the new due dates for your number one project?

Engineer: *Yes.*

Leader: Well, I'm counting on you, so make it happen!

Conversation Number 2

Leader: What concerns do you have about the accelerated due date for your number one project?

Engineer: *Plenty!*

Leader: What's the biggest concern you have about the recent change?

Engineer: *I just don't have the resources I need.*

Leader: What resources do you think you need?

Engineer: *At least two more technicians full time.*

Leader: What other options might there be?

We recognize that in this situation, adding resources may not be an acceptable option. Our approach to having a conversation does not mean you need to compromise on every issue. But you must listen to every issue. Followers in an organization often admit that they can respect a leader who thoughtfully declines their requests as long as *their leader listened to them.*

KEY THOUGHT
The centerpiece of our listening approach is to ask questions that are:

1. Open-ended

2. Vertical

3. Begin with the word "What"

Putting together the tenets of *What You Don't Know About Listening (Could Fll a Book)* will take practice.

Do not complete this chapter, walk into your most conflicted relationship, and expect to master the most favorable conversation

of your life. We recommend first practicing the skills and behaviors covered in each chapter. Then practice the combination of skills to master the entire approach.

Start Practicing

So now it's time to find someone you can practice with. We suggest that you make the learning transparent—pick a person with whom you have a good relationship and where the prospect of collateral damage is low. Tell them that you are practicing some new skills that you have learned. Ask if it would it be okay if you practiced with them.

Most will be agreeable and even give you feedback that will help you learn faster. Occasionally someone will discourage you from making the change. "You are fine the way you are," they'll say gratuitously. Thank them and move on. They may have many motives for steering you away from this change. Don't let it happen. Find yourself a different guinea pig to help you modify and reinforce your improved behavior. You can't just *think* about a behavior change, you must practice the change.

Be patient with yourself. For some, the change will be comfortable and the results will come quickly. For others, it can take some time. You may not reap the fruits of your efforts at first. But don't stop practicing until you are rewarded with a good outcome...*a markedly improved conversation!*

We taught Steve, one of our associates, the tenets of *What You Don't Know About Listening* and he found personal success almost immediately. Steve spends a lot of time on the road which definitely impacts his family life. When he learned our approach to listening, he immediately implemented the skills during his nightly calls home.

Steve's Story

I would call home every night and spend a few minutes on the phone with my daughter. I'd ask her if she had fun today, or whether she liked school that day. Without fail, I would get the same monosyllabic answers and then she'd quickly pass the phone back to her mother.

Once I learned the skills necessary to really listen, I started asking open-ended questions like, "What did you like at school today?" or "What made today a good day?"

I gradually learned that even a good question might not get a lengthy response, so I practiced being patient, letting one gentle question follow another. In time, I didn't even let a short response throw me off. I was persistent.

These nightly conversations enriched my relationship with my daughter while I was away, but also when I was home. The high-quality conversations we have today are built on that very foundation.

Steve has now shared this approach with thousands of leaders.

Change doesn't always come easily or quickly. The best way to ensure your success is to practice. Now try your hand at some exercises that can help you master listening.

Chapter Summary

- Practice open-ended, vertical questions that begin with "What."

- Be patient. When there isn't a lengthy response, gently ask another open-ended question.

- In time, people will come to sense that you really want to listen.

SKILL-BUILDING EXERCISES

1. **Putting It Together.** The purpose of this exercise is to practice putting the characteristics of a good question together to improve your listening skills. Ask a willing partner to have a conversation with you for about 15 minutes. Choose one of the conversation-starters below to begin the conversation. Don't forget, your purpose is to practice using open-ended, vertical, and "what" questions.

   Conversation-Starters:

   - What is one thing you are really proud of professionally?
   - What is something about your work history that most people don't know?
   - What is something that you are excited about at work right now?
   - What makes you happy at work?
   - What do you really appreciate about your work?

   Debrief:

   - Ask the person you listened to, to give you feedback on how well you did in terms of using open-ended, vertical and "What" questions.
   - What open-ended questions did you use?
   - How many levels deep did you get using vertical questions?
   - How successful were you at using "What" questions?
   - What did the conversation feel like for you and for the person being listened to?
   - What did you do well?

- What do you still need to improve?
- What was different or the same about this conversation compared to conversations you "normally" have?

2. **Prepare for A "Hot Topic".** The goal of this exercise is to help you put all of the characteristics of a good question into practice. To do that, it's essential to prepare. Think of an issue that you need to discuss with a peer, colleague, or subordinate. (Remember our earlier warning—don't try to tackle your most challenging issue first. Instead, pick a topic and a willing partner so you can practice your new skills in a safe environment and gain confidence in your ability.) Take some time to answer the following questions to help you better prepare for that conversation.

Prepare for the Conversation:

a. What is the topic you want to discuss?

b. What is the objective of having this conversation?

c. What do you hope to gain?

d. What does the other person have to gain in having this conversation with you?

e. What open-ended, vertical, and unbiased "What" questions can you use to begin and sustain the conversation?

f. What challenges do you anticipate?

g. What do you need to do more of—or less of—throughout this conversation to ensure its success?

h. What are potential triggers for you? What may agitate you or take you out of the conversation? What can you do to manage these triggers proactively?

_____

_____

_____

_____

_____

_____

_____

_____

Part II:
Some More Stuff
You Need to Know

7

Push Pause to Listen

By now, you know why asking questions is important, what a great question looks like (it's open-ended, vertical, and uses the word "What"), and *how* to put a great question together.

Clearly, we want to encourage you to use effective behaviors that both convey the impression that you are truly listening AND **actually force you to listen** at the same time.

KEY THOUGHT
An important factor in learning how to ask great questions is learning how to slow down and pause.

A slight gap before you speak affords you time to think for a moment…time to ponder the next great question. It's simple really—less talk equals more listening which, as you already know, means asking more great questions!

Okay, you say…so I'm going to pause. Now what am I supposed to do while I'm pausing?

Well, first you'll need to resist the temptation to immediately respond with your own statement. *Just stay quiet.* This instruction applies to introverts as well as extroverts. It's true that extroverts tend to respond—even interrupt—with multiple statements while listening. But you can bet that introverts are doing the same thing—they just don't say their thoughts out loud. The skills found here are useful whether your preference is for extroversion or introversion.

So, the bottom line here is that you will need to show restraint. Let's go back to our friends at MRG for a definition of restraint:

> **Restraint:** *Maintaining a low-key, understated, and quiet interpersonal demeanor by working to control your emotional expression.*

We like this definition and we think it goes beyond controlling your emotional expressions. It means controlling your thinking as well. Thus the pause! You'll need to keep your mind quiet for a few moments so you can ask yourself these questions:

The 4 W's

1. **What is the objective of my involvement?**

2. **Who is this person I'm talking to?**

3. **When is the right time to say something?**

4. **Where should this conversation take place?**

Question 1: What?

Ask yourself, "*What* is the objective of my involvement?" And then decide whether the "What" is important enough to address.

Not long ago we had the carpets in our office cleaned. We've used a series of vendors to clean our carpets over the years but never really found one we wanted to have back a second time. We were hoping this vendor would be different. The job was done satisfactorily, but the vendor needed to use our electrical power and the energy demand kept popping our circuit breaker. After the workers left, we discovered that the electrical socket they had been using was malfunctioning. We weren't sure what the problem was, but we were certain it had something to do with the vendor misusing our power.

We called the owner of the company to report our concern and he became immediately defensive. It was clear that the conversation was not going to go well. He was anticipating, correctly, that we wanted him to pay for any necessary repairs, and he didn't want that responsibility.

This is a Good Time to Pause.

WHAT was our objective? Well, there were a few:

1. Get the electricity restored (and yeah, that was definitely important enough to address.)
2. Minimize our cost for any repair
3. Identify a vendor we could rely upon regularly to clean our carpets to our satisfaction

This **pause** helped us realize that the third objective could result in a win-win for *both* of us.

To overcome his immediate negative reaction to our call, we explained that our intention was to create a long-term relationship with this vendor. He wanted that outcome as much as we did.

We then asked for his help in resolving our short-term problem... no electricity.

Now he was more relaxed. He led us through a power test so we could diagnose the problem. This confirmed that the outlet itself was the problem...not something more serious.

Now that the problem had a more finite resolution, the vendor felt more comfortable offering to cover the cost of repair. The repair was made and the vendor sent us a reimbursement check.

In retrospect, we recognize that our lack of electrical knowledge contributed to the vendor's immediate defensiveness. When he heard us say, *"We have an electrical problem and it was caused by your company,"* he probably had $$$$$ signs exploding inside his brain!

If we had explained our long-term goal first and then described the condition without accusing his company, we may have avoided his initial negative response.

So it's important to show restraint and determine the objective of your conversation while you are in the "pause" mode.

What if Your Objective Isn't to Reach a Consensual Conclusion?

If your objective is to prove a point or win an argument with the use of *persuasion*, then you don't need to seek the other person's input to gain a consensual decision. In this case, using your listening skills may not be important since different behaviors are in play.

But if you are interested in arriving at a consensual conclusion, as we were with our carpet cleaner, then employing listening behaviors is imperative. Let's compare the use of *persuasive* behaviors to that of *consensual* behaviors to drive this point home.

Here are MRG's definitions of these two terms.

Persuasive: *Building commitment by convincing others and winning them over to your point of view.*

Consensual: *Valuing the ideas and opinions of others and collecting their input as part of your decision-making process.*

So, think again…what is your objective? If it's to *persuade*, then perhaps exhibiting logic will be of help. In the carpet cleaning story we just recounted, we could have been quite persuasive if, from the start, we told the vendor that he would lose all future business and good word-of-mouth if he didn't pay for the costs associated with our power problem. Our point-of-view would certainly be logical; if they were responsible for breaking something, they should pay to fix it, right? But if the vendor wouldn't be persuaded and instead became defensive, we'd risk our reimbursement for the cost of the repair plus any future use of his services.

If instead, your objective is to find a consensual resolution to an issue, employing listening skills is vital in obtaining that objective. By collecting the vendor's input, we identified a win-win plan that led to him covering the cost of repairs and establishing a good relationship for ongoing carpet service.

Question 2: Who?

Think now, "*Who* exactly is this person I am talking to?" Does the relationship you have with them change your objective? Does knowing that they are a boss, peer, friend, or foe change what you'd want to say?

Imagine that you have three different employees with an attendance problem you'd like to rectify. How might the approach to your objective change in each of these situations?

Employee #1: A relatively new employee. You've never addressed this problem with them before.

Employee #2: A longer service employee who hasn't ever had an attendance problem before and is an effective contributor to your team.

Employee #3: A long-term employee to whom you have spoken before but have not seen any improvement to date.

Here's Our Take...

Employee #1: We'd want to know what this employee understands about our expectations for attendance.

Employee #2: We'd want to support this employee if something has changed in their work or life.

Employee #3: Depending on the conversations that we've had with this employee in the past and consistent with the policies of our company, we may want to move this individual into progressive discipline.

Would the amount of listening change in each of these situations? Absolutely.

Question 3: When?

Think about this. "*When* is the right time to say something?" Is this really the best time to achieve your objective or could there be a better time? Here are some things to consider:

- **Is there too much adrenaline flowing through your veins (or theirs) right now?**

- **Do you have enough information to have an effective conversation?**

- **How has this person reacted to similar situations in the past?**

In the wake of these questions, a key bit of advice is to have the conversation *as soon as possible*. Does that mean right now? Not necessarily. If emotions are running high, wait a bit. Either put the thought aside for a moment, or write it down on a sheet of paper. The person may be more receptive to what you want to say at a later time, and in the meantime you'll be able to think about alternative ways to communicate your message. That said, have the conversation soon so the context is not diluted by time.

As executive coaches, we often use a 360-degree survey process to provide feedback to our clients. Through instruments and personal interviews, we learn how bosses, peers and direct reports perceive the executive with whom we are working.

To deliver the collected feedback results to that executive, we schedule two meetings, a week apart. The first meeting is devoted to sharing the information in a way that clarifies our client's strengths and weaknesses.

Near the end of the first meeting we can discern *when* this particular individual may be ready to discuss behavioral changes. Most often, they'll need time to reflect on what they have heard. Waiting more than a week to have the second meeting, though, would be a mistake. They need just enough time between the two meetings to carefully consider the information they've learned, and then clear their head so they can stand back and identify perceptions they accept versus those that they don't yet understand.

Always ask yourself this question: **When** is the best time to achieve the **what** (or objective) of this conversation?

Question 4: Where?

Ask, "*Where* should I have this conversation?" Is it OK to do this in public or might it be better if you were in a more private location?

We suggest that anything other than a casual conversation should be planned for a space that could provide privacy if it becomes necessary.

A Story from Jon

Unfortunately, early in my career, I learned this lesson the hard way. I needed to clear the air with a colleague in conjunction with preparing to deliver their annual review. I thought a relaxed and friendly atmosphere would enhance the process, so I extended an invitation for lunch.

It was a 30-minute drive to the restaurant and we struck up a very pleasant conversation along the way.

Then, once our food was delivered to the table, I began to outline the areas of concern that we should discuss. The conversation spiraled downward rapidly, and though we hadn't raised our voices, neighboring diners could probably feel the chill that enveloped the table.

The 30-minute ride back to work was the longest—and the quietest—ride I've ever taken. I learned a very valuable "where" lesson that day.

KEY THOUGHT

Having an important conversation in the wrong environment can undo all of the other listening skills that you bring to the interaction.

So, when a discussion begins, learn to **PAUSE** and ask yourself the **4 W's: What, Who, When and Where.**

This may take some practice. The PAUSE may seem awkward at first, but you'll find that with practice, you'll process the 4 W's more and more quickly. Your reward? A conversation filled with great questions that is productive, consensual, builds trust, and furthers the work at hand.

Here's an example... ﹀

Let's take the employee attendance problem from a few pages ago and run it all the way through the **4 W's.** We'll assume it's a long service employee and that we've discussed this issue with them previously.

Manager: When would be a good time for us to have a chat in my office? **(When/Where)**

Employee: *Right now will be fine.*

Manager: I've noticed that you've had a string of absences again. What can you tell me about your situation? **(What)**

Employee: *Well, it's a personal medical situation.*

Manager: I can understand that you may not want to discuss something that's private. Without sharing anything personal, what can you tell me about when you'll be back to full time? **(What)**

Employee: *I'm not sure.*

Manager: May I share something with you?

Employee: *Of course.*

Manager: I know you're saying "yes," but I want to be sure you are okay with me being totally honest.

Employee: *Yes I am.*

Manager: You are a long service employee. **(Who)** I appreciate that. This last year you have been absent 30% of the time. I cannot consider you a full-time employee at that rate. Your absence makes it impossible to schedule our work flow. Unless you can give me a reasonable expectation that this will change, I need to consider ending your employment with us.

Caution: Be sure to work with your HR representative to ensure you are following company policy and state laws before taking this kind of action.

Chapter Summary

- Learn how to pause in order to prepare to ask great questions

- Ask yourself:

    » WHAT is my objective

    » WHO am I talking to

    » WHEN is the right time to say something and

    » WHERE should we have this conversation

8

Offering Your Opinion

Okay, okay, after all this listening, we know you're working up a hunger to express your extremely valuable opinion. But wait a minute…as brilliant as it probably is, do you *really* need to put in your two cents?

If the conversation has gone well, could you get all the results that you want by simply thanking them for their input and endorsing an action or idea they have expressed? Hey, we're all for getting out while you're ahead.

But if you just can't help yourself, this chapter is meant to provide you with the mechanisms to transition from listening to *sharing* your thoughts. Just follow these three steps.

1. **Decide if the "When" Should Be RIGHT NOW?**
    If the conversation has broken down and emotions are running high on either side of the table, it's probably better to suspend the conversation for the moment. The other person most likely has no appetite for your thoughts right now—and

you may be too amped up to share them. Also, one of you may need more time to collect pertinent information so you can have a future meaningful conversation.

2. **Pause.**

Recognize that this may not go well if you charge ahead. Decide whether that's okay. If not, you might say, *"Thank you for sharing that information. You gave me a lot to think about. Let's get together again tomorrow to discuss this some more. What time works best for you?"*

How often has an interaction been improved after you have walked away and calmed down? How many relationships have been preserved by someone collecting their thoughts, gathering data, or clarifying their objectives for the conversation?

But don't use this as an excuse to procrastinate. If it's your cowardly attempt to ignore the situation or indefinitely postpone the rest of the conversation, chances are you'll have to start all over again...and it may be harder the second time around. If you wait too long, feelings may calcify and you'll have an impenetrable wall to knock down before you can share your thoughts. Let the heat simmer down, but don't wait too long.

3. **Hurrah! The Conversation is Going Well.**

Now can I share my opinion? Well...not quite yet. First you must ask for permission.

KEY THOUGHT

Ask permission to share your thoughts—a person who has given you permission is more likely to stay engaged in the process and committed to the outcome.

What's Behind the Asking for Permission?

Psychologically, a person who has given you permission to give your opinion is more likely to stay engaged in the process. By offering that person some measure of control (hard as it may be for you), you increase the likelihood that they will be more open to listening and committed to the outcome of the conversation.

On the other hand, if you plunge in with your unsolicited opinion, you could undo all of the benefit you have derived from using your **open-ended, vertical, "What" questions.** When you force your opinion on another person, they may appear to give passive acceptance to your thoughts, but passive—as in passive aggressive—is not a good thing, is it? For maximum success, you need to get them onboard *before* providing your feedback. Asking for permission helps accomplish that.

You may feel this approach isn't assertive enough. You're thinking that your rank, your expertise, or your emotions give you the authority to push ahead— it doesn't matter whether or not anyone's ready to hear you.

Be assured that, in most cases, we believe it's important for you to share your point of view…we just want to help you deliver it in a way that it is more likely to be heard.

When you ask for permission to share your opinions, we have found there are three typical responses:

- **Ninety percent** of the time they will give you that permission and you can proceed.

- **Nine percent** of the time they will give you permission, but you may need to clarify your reasons for asking permission and, once you've done that, you should request their permission a second time.

- **One percent** of the time they will deny you permission. We'll explain how to deal with that rarity before the end of this chapter.

For the 90% Who Said "Yes"

Because you have given the other person control by asking for permission, we think their sense of ownership in the conversation's outcome will double. What's more, *you will magnify their motivation to make that outcome successful.*

Here's an example of a good permission question. Notice that it starts with positive reinforcement for their ideas:

"I really appreciate you sharing this information with me. I liked several of your ideas for accelerating the project. May I share some additional thoughts with you?"

For that Nine Percent We Mentioned

In these cases, you've gotten permission to share your point of view, but you realize that what you are about to share is likely to produce a defensive reaction. You should rearticulate your request because you need to be crystal clear about your motives for delivering this information.

We assume that your intentions are not to hurt or demotivate the other person. But if your input is perceived as criticism, it could easily be taken as a direct attack. Pause. What is your motive?

Often, your intention is to share a perception (or fact) of which they may not be aware. You know that unless they are informed of this observation, they won't be able to perform as they—or you— would like. It isn't fair to withhold data that affects their future. **You have an *obligation* to share this information** so that they have the opportunity to refute it. Perhaps they can change your perception by taking corrective actions.

Here's how you could communicate your message:

Taken from a Performance Review Conversation

> *"Thank you for agreeing to hear my thoughts. I want you to know that they may make you uncomfortable. That being said, I feel I must share them with you. They are based on a perception I have and I believe it's unfair to keep this perception from you. Unless we discuss it, you won't have the awareness or the option to change my perception. So, are you sure you are okay with my sharing these thoughts with you?"*

With this approach, you have made your motives clear. The serious tone may unfortunately increase the tension in the room, but what can we say, this is serious business. Might the person still be defensive? Probably. There's nothing that can thwart this basic animal reaction. Will this approach lead to more open conversations, you ask? Yes, absolutely.

For the Rare One Percent

Seldom, if ever, will someone refuse to hear your opinion. If they do, you should realize that the objective of the conversation has just shifted. It's no longer about Topic A. You can't talk about Topic A because something is so wrong in this relationship that the person doesn't even want to hear your opinion.

In this case, you might say something like this:

You: "I really appreciate you sharing this information with me. May I share some of my thoughts with you?"

Them: *"No."*

You: "What is it that stands in the way of us having this conversation?"

To learn more about having these specific types of conversations, turn to our Chapter 19, "Overcoming Conflict."

For the 99% who are open to hearing your opinion (that's all but the one percent discussed above), we have a few more tips.

- Many leaders tend to dump all their concerns, good advice, and right answers on the other person. This may gain you their compliance, but you will likely fall short of getting their commitment. Try to focus on the one or two concerns that are critical.

- If you regularly follow your request for permission with something that either negates what they have said or "proves" your role as the expert who has all the "right answers", eventually—even if they grant permission for you to share your thoughts—you'll notice the mental light switch turning off. You can keep talking but they'll be taking a 30-second listening vacation.

- Occasionally follow your request for permission with a positive thought (when it's merited, of course). It's amazing how powerful a bit of praise can be. It can virtually neutralize the potential for forming a negative neuro-linguistic connection whenever you ask to share your thoughts. Regularly asking permission to share either positive or negative feedback will prevent your requests from being "programmed" into something that is automatically seen as bad.

- Don't combine positive and negative feedback in the same sentence by using "but" as a transition from one to the other. Simply end the sentence with the positive comment and start a new sentence without that conjunction. We instinctively respond to the word "but" in a negative way.

KEY THOUGHT

If you only provide criticisms every time you ask to share your thoughts, you will establish a new neuro-linguistic connection that may subliminally cause a negative or defensive reaction in the other person.

Would you be surprised to learn that many leaders seldom give positive feedback? Didn't think so. In view of that, here are some examples to help you get started.

An employee has just described the actions she took to generate an important report for you.

You: "May I share my thoughts with you?"

Them: *"Yes."*

You: "You really did a great job on that report. I'm truly proud of you. I appreciated your attention to detail and the hours you spent to make it stand out from the competition."

In this example, we are providing more than a compliment. Mentioning the "attention to detail" and the "hours you spent" shows that you were actually listening to her description of the task. This makes the compliment more powerful. Praise without specifics like these often feels empty to the recipient.

The compliment could go even deeper in the form of an *acknowledgment*, the distinction being that an acknowledgment gets to the heart of who the other person is as much as what they've done. A simple acknowledgment may be all the other person needs to boost their confidence, stand a little taller and thus believe they can succeed in the next task ahead. For those high achievers on your team who only need a little boost, this may be the right antidote. In this case, the message may sound something like:

You: "May I share my thoughts with you?"

Them: *"Yes."*

You: "You really showed your commitment to the team during that meeting. You took a big risk, and I know that was hard for you. You stood up for your values and your authenticity really paid off. Great job!"

You could also decide to challenge them to think about a problem differently by providing an example of a similar scenario you faced, or by providing them with alternative questions that they should further explore. Your conversation could go like this:

You: "May I share my thoughts with you?"

Them: *"Yes."*

You: "As I said, I liked several of your ideas for accelerating the project. I encourage you to put special emphasis on your suggestion for hiring that additional resource.

Or, it may sound like this:

You?   "May I share my thoughts with you?"

Them: *"Yes."*

You?   "As I said, I liked several of your ideas for accelerating the project. I faced a similar situation last May. I found that bringing the customer into the loop made all the difference. What could you do to get the customer more involved?"

Notice that we are providing positive feedback *plus* sharing our view by asking a question. We are continuing a very consensual tone in this conversation. There is no need to assert command and control with a person who is performing well.

We are not recommending that you make only positive comments. People appreciate directness. However, variation in what you say will make the comments more genuine and way less predictable.

Keep in mind, our intention is not to script what you should say; we simply want to challenge you to think about what you say and how you say it so that your conversation has the best possible outcome.

Chapter Summary

- Ask permission to share your opinions.

- Share positive thoughts as frequently as you share critiques.

- Whenever possible, do not include positive and negative comments in the very same conversation. The positive comments will not be heard.

- Vary the way in which you communicate your comments to avoid programming a negative response.

SKILL-BUILDING EXERCISES

1. **Rewind and Share Your Opinion.** The goal of this exercise is to begin shifting your behavior by practicing the skill of sharing your opinion. First, recall a recent conversation in which you provided feedback or shared your thoughts with a peer, colleague, or subordinate without asking permission to share your thoughts.

    Write out the conversation as it played out. What was the impact?

    Next, "rewind" the conversation and write out an alternative conversation. Imagine that you share your opinion by asking permission first. What is the likely impact now?

    (Important: Remember to first to consider the merit of sharing your thoughts at all, and then think about how you want to phrase what you share.)

    _____

    _____

    _____

    _____

    _____

2. **Practice Asking for Permission to Share Your Opinions.** The goal of this exercise is to practice asking permission to offer your thoughts. Find a willing partner and take a moment to have a conversation together. Make sure you ask their permission to share your thoughts. To get started, use any of the following conversation starters (or make one up on your own):

- What is a simple work habit you would like to change?
- What do you want to do more of in your work life?
- What would it look like to have a really satisfying career?
- What is a problem you are facing that you'd like to tackle?

_____

_____

_____

_____

Debrief:

- First, did you ask permission to share your thoughts?
- Ask your partner to give you feedback on how granting permission impacted their willingness to listen to your thoughts.
- Gather some feedback on the necessity and the quality level of the thoughts you chose to share.
- How did it feel to ask permission to share your thoughts?
- What was different, the same, better, and more challenging about this approach?

_____

_____

_____

_____

3. **Acknowledgment.** The goal of this exercise is expand the types of thoughts you can share with another person once you have gained their permission to share your thoughts and feedback.

- Make a list of five people at work. Write an acknowledgement of who they had to be to get where they are today. Challenge yourself and choose at least one person of whom you may need to acquire a more positive perspective...we promise, this will help.

  For example, "Sanjay, you have had to be team oriented, hard working and committed to building this business. I appreciate how you always stayed true to the vision, while evolving with the times. I know it wasn't an easy balance. I really admire how dedicated you have been to mentoring new talent, asking for fresh ideas, staying current on trends and yet always grounded in the company values."

- Take the time to write an acknowledgment for yourself.

_____

_____

_____

_____

_____

_____

_____

9

Finishing the Conversation

Closing the conversation brings the dialogue full circle. Without a proper close, you are essentially left hanging with no decisions made, no plan to work, and no sense of closure. All your listening efforts may be fruitless unless you finish strong.

So, how do you know when the conversation is over? And, what do you say to bring it to a close?

KEY THOUGHT

The duration of most conversations seems to be dictated by the clock rather than the content. Change that.

You'll know a conversation is over when there is no additional value to be gained from continuing the discussion. The clock is not relevant. Some issues will require much less than the typical 60 minutes, while others need much more than the excruciating hour.

Three ways you know your conversation should come to a close...

- **Emotions are running so high that there is no value in continuing**

- **New ideas are no longer being generated**

- **The next logical step in the conversation is to "get to work"**

If emotions are making it difficult to continue, you may find it easier to delay the remainder of the conversation. Use your judgment. Perhaps working through the emotions will be worthwhile. Don't be afraid of anger or tears if they are useful in clearing the air.

But that doesn't mean you should allow yourself to become out-of-control, nor should you put the other person in a terribly uncomfortable position. Be willing to suspend the interaction if gaining composure allows either party a chance to gather their thoughts and be more productive in the next meeting.

When you sense that you have accomplished as much as possible, simply bring it to a close. Or if it feels right to put together an action plan and begin "doing" the work, this is the place in the conversation to make that happen.

Below are the steps we find most useful in closing the conversation:

- **Thank the person**
- **Ask for their view of what has been discussed**
- **Consider asking for a plan**
- **Negotiate a follow-up date**
- **Thank the person again**

Here is what each of those steps might sound like:

Thank the Person

- *"I really appreciated the opportunity to talk with you."*

- *"Thanks for taking the time to talk with me."*

- *"Thank you for sharing your thoughts with me."*

Ask for Their View of What Has Been Discussed

- *"What key points do you take away from our conversation?"*

- *"What do you think is the best way to summarize all this?"*

- *"What is your key take-away?"*

Consider Asking for a Plan

- *"What next steps should be taken based on our conversation?"*

- *"What is the best way to proceed based on our discussion?"*

- *"What are the action steps from here?"*

- *"How do you feel about developing a plan based on our conversation?"*

Negotiate a Follow-Up Date

- *"When should we meet again to follow up this conversation?"*

- *"What is your availability next week to follow up on this conversation?"*

- *"What is the best time to meet again?"*

Thank the Person Again

- *"Once again, thank you for the opportunity to discuss this. I've learned that I need to (something that you learned that is your responsibility and does not infer the other person is to blame). I'll calendar our next meeting on XX/XX/XX."*

- *"Thanks again, I appreciate your hard work in all this. I'll do XYZ and get back to you next week."*

- *"I appreciate your support. We both have some work to do between now and next week! Thanks again."*

Don't make a commitment for an action or a future meeting and then neglect to follow through. The perception that you are a good listener is supported by your actions beyond the duration of the conversation. We all know those leaders who give lip service (or ear service) to other's ideas only to have their lack of follow-through destroy any perception that they have truly listened. Don't let that person be you!

Chapter Summary

- The length of your conversation should be determined by the content—not the clock.

- Thank the other person for participating.

- Make a plan and then follow it through.

Here are some exercises that will help you close a conversation comfortably.

SKILL-BUILDING EXERCISES

1. **The Natural End Point.** The goal of this exercise is to help you identify the natural end point of a conversation so you know when and how to close it comfortably. Think about the last three conversations or meetings you had at work. What was the end point of the conversation? Try to categorize it (e.g., too many

emotions, ran out of ideas, natural point to take action on an item). Did you make a plan? Did you agree to meet again? What was the impact of either having a good finish or a not-so-good finish to the conversation?

_____

_____

_____

_____

_____

_____

2. **Close the Conversation.** The goal of this exercise is to help you practice finishing the conversation and to ensure it is properly completed. Think about a recent conversation you had where you brainstormed or made some decisions but never "closed" the conversation. What was the impact?

    Now, take the time to imagine "closing" the conversation and finishing the dialogue. Imagine you are going to go back and talk with this person to properly close the conversation so that you can get the work back on track. Use the steps below to support you as you list your questions and responses:

    - Thank the person

    - Ask for their view of what has been discussed

    - Consider asking for a plan

- Negotiate a follow-up date
- Thank the person again

_____

_____

_____

_____

_____

_____

3. **Self-Assessment.** The goal of this exercise is to assess your strengths in creating a strong "finish" to the conversation. Think about the steps above. Which of these is your strong suit? Which do you often forget to do? What do you need to remember the next time?

_____

_____

_____

_____

_____

_____

10

Putting Everything Together

So now that you have learned the individual behaviors for good listening, you are ready to put it all together. Let's review:

1. **Pause first**—ask yourself *what, who, when and where*

2. **Ask the other person questions**—open-ended, vertical questions beginning with the word "What"

3. **Decide whether you should offer your point of view**—think about if, when, how, and what to share

4. **Close the conversation**—be sure to thank them for their participation

5. **Determine if a summary or an action plan makes sense**—who should take responsibility?

That brief list of items could represent a significant amount of behavior change for you. If it does, figure out where you need the most help. We suggest you go back and reread those portions of the book that address the skills you want to acquire and then practice those specific exercises.

Remember, practice makes permanent. You can't expect to become an instant listening expert just because you've read all our chapters. You may stumble the first few times you try to use these techniques. But if you practice them diligently, they will become second nature to you.

KEY THOUGHT
It's about a six-month process for an adult to become aware of a need to change, examine the root causes of a behavior, select new behaviors, practice those behaviors, and then sustain the new behaviors over time.

Don't be discouraged. People do it all the time. Here is the approach of one person we coached on this method. Take a look at how Roger tackled the challenge:

1. First, Roger took time to evaluate and reflect upon the type of conversations he was having. He realized he was shutting down his conversations by asking closed-ended questions.

2. He then prepared for some low-risk meetings by jotting down a few open-ended questions that began with "What." He used those to guide the conversation.

3. Afterwards, he assessed how these conversations went so he could make improvements the next time.

4. Though Roger is tough on himself when the conversation doesn't flow naturally, he found the places where his exchanges were markedly improved. That feeling of success encouraged him to use these techniques in more and more conversations with the hopes of making it all feel natural.

Step 4 above is very important. It's way too easy to give up on your new behaviors after only one or two attempts. If you see no instant reward, you won't be encouraged to continue to learn and improve. But once you have a truly effective conversation, you'll want to repeat that feeling of effectiveness again and again. Keep trying. Give yourself time to reach a comfort level and you'll find yourself using these behaviors in every conversation, whether it's at work or at home.

Chapter Summary

Practice, practice, practice!!!

For those of you feeling more confident in your ability to put it all together, use the following skill-building exercises to get your listening muscles that much more toned.

SKILL-BUILDING EXERCISES

1. **Practice Putting Everything Together.** The goal of this exercise is to help you put all the tools together to support building your listening skills. During this exercise we want you to practice using open-ended, vertical, "What" questions along with asking to share your thoughts when appropriate.

   Think of someone at work who has recently come to you with a problem they want to solve together. Take the time to prepare for that conversation. Use the following questions to help you prepare for the conversation:

   a. Who is it you need to have a conversation with?

   b. What is the objective, intention or purpose of this conversation?

c. What do you have to gain?

d. What does the other person have to gain?

e. What is the nature of the "problem" they have presented?

f. When is the right time to have this conversation?

g. Where should you have this conversation?

h. What are the open-ended, vertical, "What" questions that you could use to begin the conversation?

i. What are the open-ended, vertical, "What" questions that may stimulate you and the other person to think differently about the problem?

j. If appropriate, what thoughts do you want to share and what is best way to ask permission to share them?

k. What is the likely impact of sharing your advice or thoughts in this conversation?

l. Do you anticipate meeting again? If so, how can you effectively close this conversation to ensure that you are prepared for your next meeting?

_____

_____

_____

_____

_____

_____

2. **Role-Play.** The goal of this exercise is to practice having the problem-solving conversation you just prepared for in the previous exercise. Find a willing partner. First brief them on the elements you planned for, giving them a small background on the person they are role-playing and how you anticipate that person to react. Once you are both prepared, take about ten minutes to have the conversation. Use the following questions to help you debrief:

- Ask your Partner to provide feedback on how well you, the Listener, succeeded in:

  » Asking open-ended, vertical, and "What" questions.

  » Asking permission to share your opinion and the quality of feedback or thoughts you chose to share.

- What open-ended, vertical, and "What" questions did you ask?

- How did the person being listened to feel about the conversation?

- How did you feel about the conversation?

- What did you do particularly well?

- What opportunities still exist for improvement?

- What was the overall impact or result of the conversation?

- What do you still need to do to prepare for your "real-life" conversation?

_____

_____

_____

3. **Self-Management.** The goal of this exercise is to identify where you are most likely to get hung up in the next conversation that requires you to truly listen. Where are you likely to get sidetracked in the midst of the conversation? Where are you probably going to need self-management?

    *   List ten things that your conversation partner could do or say that would cause you to want to step aside from using open-ended, vertical, unbiased "What" questions. In other words, what would make you want to stop listening? *(Think about what would make you get angry, try to persuade, lose confidence in yourself, try to problem-solve, go into judgment, start to defend a position, try to provide advice too early...etc.?)*

    *   Next, list ten things that you could do to return to the conversation and stay in listening mode.

4. **Asking Permission.** The goal of this exercise is to flex those "asking permission" muscles so you can feel more comfortable when asking permission to share your thoughts. Asking permission is one of the powerful ways we remind ourselves and the other person that they are in charge of themselves and have a measure of control in the conversation. The added benefit is that we help to keep the other person engaged in listening to our feedback. It also can prevent us from becoming aggressive or remaining too passive. It helps us better embody a collaborative or assertive way of being. We are more poised to listen.

Make a list of five different ways you can ask permission to provide feedback, offer an opinion, or share your thoughts.

Some examples:

- *"May I share my thoughts with you?"*

- *"May we spend some time working on this issue together?"*

- *"Would you like some feedback on that?"*

- *"May I tell you what I see about the way you are handling this?*

- *"May I give you a challenge?"*

- *"May I share some advice with you?"*

- *"May I share a personal experience with you that may be relevant here?"*

- *May I tell you some of the feedback I've collected about your performance?"*

- *"May I make a request?"*

Now, write down five additional ways you could ask permission to share your thoughts.

_____

_____

_____

_____

_____

_____

_____

_____

5. **Conversation Starter.** The goal of this exercise is to help you put all your listening skills together. Here is a quick reminder of each of the skills:

> **Pause** − *Ask yourself what, who, when and where*
>
> **Ask the other person questions** − *Open-ended, vertical questions beginning with the word "What"*
>
> **Decide whether to offer your point of view** − *Think about if, when, how and what to share*
>
> **Close the conversation** − *Thank the other person*
>
> **Determine if either a summary or action plan make sense** − *Who should take responsibility?*

First, ask a willing partner to have a 15-minute conversation with you. Use any one of the following conversation starters to begin.

- What are you worried about right now at work?

- What do you do when you get stressed?

- What is a risk you recently took at work that turned out well?

- What is a professional goal you have for yourself right now?

- What is a secret career dream that you have?

Debrief:

- How did the conversation feel?

- What happened when you paused? What facets of the conversation improved?

- What was the impact of using open-ended, vertical, and "What" questions?

- What impact did asking permission to share your thoughts have?

- Did you close the conversation or determine an action plan? What was the impact?

- What did you do well overall?

- What do you still need to work on?

The following chapters discuss how you can apply all you've learned to the leadership challenges you commonly face, such as seeking feedback, hiring, onboarding, coaching, reviewing performance, decision-making, delegating, leading change and overcoming conflict. These chapters are filled with real-life stories, examples, and more skill-building exercises to help you get these new competencies "into your bones". We encourage you to keep practicing!

Part III:
What It All Sounds
Like When You Are...

11

Seeking Feedback

A Story from Jon

The first time I was the subject of a formal 360-degree feedback process, I was shocked by the outcome. My scores for persuasive behavior were very high; but even worse, my consensual scores were low. And, because I had answered the questions as honestly as I could, I guess it shouldn't have been a surprise that my own scores agreed with those of all the participating observers.

*At first I was in denial because I thought I could remember each and every situation where I had surfaced the opinions of others. "Well, of course," I rationalized. "Being a turn-around specialist necessitates lightening quick and effective action. I probably didn't have the time to seek out **every person's** input."*

But in time, I came to accept that this was not the style of leadership that I wanted to be branded with, and I also suspected it would limit my success.

Why was I unaware of this perception? And if I actually had scored myself in this fashion, why was I in denial at first? Then the simple answer occurred to me—I hadn't been regularly seeking feedback from my "customers."

KEY THOUGHT

Your boss, your peers, and your direct reports are "customers" of your leadership.

We've all been asked to participate in customer feedback surveys. Research has demonstrated that companies can strengthen customer loyalty—and thus preserve revenue—by asking for the opinions of those who buy their goods and services.

Leadership is the commodity you provide. Doesn't it make sense for you to uncover the true perceptions that these customers of your Leadership possess?

So why do leaders avoid doing this? Do any of these excuses sound familiar?

- **You don't have the time**

- **You think that admitting a mistake is a sign of weakness**

- **Or maybe you *truly think* that others are less capable than you**

And what price are you paying for these excuses? Much more than you think because:

- **You'll appear less curious and less open to learning and self-improvement**

- **You'll model that same *"resistance to learning"* for others**

- **Your apparent lack of curiosity may raise a question about your ability to take on more challenging assignments**

- **You'll dampen any enthusiasm for teamwork**

Yes, we said teamwork. We are beginning to understand that promoting feedback within an organization has the ability to transform a culture and significantly improve team effectiveness.

Dan Wilson, from the Harvard Graduate School of Education and a researcher with Project Zero, has done a lot of fieldwork on high-performance teams. He asserts that this one regular behavior, seeking feedback, will help to promote collaborative behaviors in the rest of the team. He found that high-performance teams do this 80% of the time, versus 20-30% in low-performance teams.

So, how do you seek feedback? No surprise here—you ask lots of questions!

A Word of Warning

If you seek feedback, but then react defensively to the candid response you receive, it's unlikely you will get honest data from that point forward.

A Story from Alexandra

In the hundreds of leadership seminars that I have taught, giving and receiving feedback is very often a part of the training, as it is an essential skill for leaders to acquire. Always, the greater challenge is in receiving the feedback. When someone tells you that there's something you don't do well, it's easy to become defensive. I maintain that feedback is a gift, and the only appropriate response is "thank you." Even if you don't like the feedback, you can thank them for having the courage to be honest with you.

One particular leader I worked with would always make excuses for her behavior whenever she received feedback. During our coaching she would say, "That's just their opinion." As an objective observer, I could see this wasn't just one person's opinion but the perception of many. I asked her if she was willing to participate in a 360-degree feedback review. This can reveal patterns that make it clear that a perception is consistent across multiple respondents—not just one person's opinion.

For this leader, the impact was profound. Everyone agreed that she had "bad habits", and now that she knew that everyone knew, she was more willing to admit to her failings. It was a relief for everyone! She found it somewhat paradoxical—when she admitted that she wasn't perfect, her team gained more respect for her. Rather than think less of her, they valued her more.

So recognize the gift you receive when someone cares enough about you to give you feedback. Remember, too, that it's a gift that keeps on giving (once you decide to do something about what was shared!)

If you want to repeatedly gather leadership feedback, leave your own opinions out of the conversation. Imagine, for example, that you told a restaurant manager that your meal was poorly prepared and were met with the accusation that you didn't eat their food in the right way. How frustrated and angry would you feel? So if you want to succeed in receiving valuable input from your "customers", simply seek the feedback, thank them, find something that will drive a useful change, and then act on it.

These are three examples of good Feedback conversations. Keep in mind that here, your "customer" could be your boss, your peers, or your direct reports.

Scenario 1

Leader: I'm interested in improving the leadership I provide. What's one thing that you think I could do differently?

Martin: *I'm not sure what you mean.*

Leader: Well, there's probably something that I do that makes it more difficult for you to be successful. I'd like to become more aware of that and see if I can make changes that could better support you.

Martin: *Well...sometimes you throw stuff at me last minute and it disrupts my day.*

Leader: Thank you for sharing that feedback. I can see that it would be frustrating to get assignments at the last minute. What would you see as ideal?

Scenario 2

Leader: One of my personal goals is to continue to improve my leadership. What's one thing I can change for the better?

Rosa: *I don't know. You're pretty great.*

Leader: Thanks for the compliment, but nobody's perfect. What can I do better?

Rosa: *I sometimes feel like you manage more than you need to. Maybe we could look at some of the projects and figure out how to delegate responsibilities.*

Leader: Thank you, I appreciate your honesty. I think that sounds like a great idea.

Scenario 3

Leader: What feedback do you have for me?

Amir: *I would like to see you be more assertive in our management meetings.*

Leader: Okay. May I ask specifically what you have in mind, so I know I'm on the right track?

Amir: *Yes, I'd like you to begin to drive the meetings and take a more active role in managing the brainstorming and decision process.*

Leader: Thanks, I appreciate the feedback. I'll make a commitment to work on that. May I continue to seek your feedback on the progress I'm making?

What do you do with the information you gather? We recognize that you may not be able to address every perception your "customers" have, but you may be able to start by making *one significant change that is felt by those around you.*

If you haven't requested feedback from your team in the past, you may want to lower your expectations at first. Because you have positional power over those who report to you, it will take time for them to realize that you sincerely want their input.

So, if seeking feedback is something new for you, choose the time and place to initiate this behavior carefully. Don't ask for feedback spontaneously, or while you're angry, or in public. It's important to carefully think through the objective of the conversation. Be sure that your attitude can remain positive no matter what is said. And select a location that does not represent your power. For example, don't choose your own office with you seated behind your desk. A private, neutral conference room is a good choice. A hallway or coffee shop is not.

Here's what the Feedback-Giver Requires:

1. You should create a comfortable and trusting atmosphere. They must have confidence that there won't be any negative consequences for their candor. They have to be able to trust you on this.

2. You must sincerely take all comments seriously. Your direct reports will help you grow if their opinions are valued and they are personally respected. Will they require you to act on everything that's said? No. But will they expect you to change in some meaningful way? YES.

Your boss or your peers may open up sooner than a direct report might. You could practice this behavior on them before you try to go to a direct report. Just be sure to listen!

Developing a high feedback culture takes time. If you can ensure that all the conditions we've mentioned are in place, then you'll find that the quality and quantity of your feedback will continue to increase.

An Update from Jon

As my denial about not being consensual dissipated, I began a journey to explore how I might adapt my leadership to change how others perceived me. Over time, I began to realize that listening is a core behavior that supports the perception that one is cooperative, consensual and empathetic. This realization improved my leadership and my teamwork. (You will have to ask my writing partner if I've made any progress!)

What I learned along the way became the seeds that, with Alexandra's help, have grown into this book.

Chapter Summary

- When you seek feedback, you're employing the same techniques as a business that asks for their customers' feedback. Your boss, peers, and direct reports are customers of your leadership.

- If you seek feedback, but then react defensively to the candid response you receive, it's unlikely you will get honest data from that point forward.

- Research indicates that when a leader seeks feedback, they can increase their team's effectiveness.

- We recommend saying "thank you" for the feedback, and then acting on it.

Here are some exercises to help you get started on your journey.

SKILL-BUILDING EXERCISES

1. **Start, Stop, Continue.** The goal of this exercise is to help you gain a greater comfort level with seeking and receiving feedback.

   - Think of someone at work who you could comfortably ask for feedback. Ask them to give you feedback on three things:
     - » Things you can start doing to be more effective
     - » Things you can stop doing to be more effective
     - » Things you should continue doing to be more effective

   - Next, thank them for the feedback. Then make a commitment to do something about one of the pieces of feedback they have given you.

_____

_____

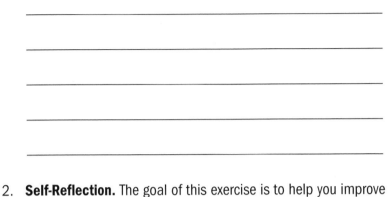

2. **Self-Reflection.** The goal of this exercise is to help you improve your ability to receive feedback. First, reflect on past feedback you've received. Write down a list of 3-5 things your customers (direct reports, boss, or peers) have told you could be improved. Next, write down what you have done or not done to change that behavior for the better. What is the impact of your action or inaction? What do you need to do going forward?

3. **Feedback is a Gift.** The goal of this exercise is to help you practice receiving feedback. At the end of each meeting you have over the next week, ask your meeting partner if there is anything you can do better or differently as it relates to your work together. Practice thanking each person for the feedback. Notice the patterns that emerge; who is willing to provide you with feedback (or not willing to provide it)? What do you notice? Is there something you are doing to impact their level of honesty with you? What do you want to do with the feedback you have received to date? If you act on it, what will the impact be? How are you feeling about receiving so much feedback? What do you have to lose or gain?

12

Hiring

A Story from Jon

The worst interview I ever participated in (as a candidate) was with the president of a manufacturing company. This business was struggling and the president knew that the success of any attempted turnaround rested squarely on the shoulders of his new hire. If I got this job, I'd be responsible for saving the company.

The president had seen my resume ahead of time. He must have determined based on the experience listed, that I was more than qualified for the position.

The interview lasted an hour and a half, but I do not remember being asked one question. He spent a small portion of the time describing the position's challenges and the rest of the time he recounted stories of the heroics he had performed to keep the company afloat.

At the end of the interview I was offered the job! Come on!

There was no way that I was going to work for someone who couldn't listen, so I declined the offer.

This story may seem extreme, but think about all the interviews you've witnessed in your career. Interview questions are usually just a rehash of the data found in the resume, and they are likely to be activity-based. "What did you do, then what did you do next, etc." How about this famous question that has no depth whatsoever; "Tell me about yourself?" Questions like these have no chance of getting to the critical issues and key success factors identified for the role.

This approach may be fine for initial screenings, but it just doesn't cut it for final interviews. **You need to ask the questions that help you determine whether the candidate has *what matters* most to the role for which you are hiring.** Consider reviewing Chapter 4, "Vertical Questions" in Part One for a refresher on how to do this.

KEY THOUGHT
Use vertical questions to determine how candidates really think and to predict how they will act in the position.

Avoid expensive mistakes when you conduct an interview; always make listening a priority. Studies from respected organizations such as Harvard University, the Corporate Leadership Council, and the National Human Resources organization all concur that up to 80% of employee turnover stems from mistakes made during the hiring process.[1]

High turnover can be expensive. "The cost to replace and hire new staff is estimated to be 60 percent of an employee's

---

1   Adriana, Costello, "The True Cost of Employee Turnover," March 29, 2012, www.hr.com.

annual salary, according to a Society for Human Resources Foundation report. And total costs of replacement, including training and loss of productivity, can range from 90 percent to 200 percent of an employee's annual salary, according to a PricewaterhouseCoopers white paper."[2] You do the math—turnover is not cheap! And these numbers don't take into account the soft costs of a bad hire, like the emotional toll it can take on a group's morale, or the reduction in an organization's effectiveness.

Now, think of the situations where our "Billy Badhire" is allowed to remain in his position, even though he's clearly not performing successfully. Okay, maybe he's not a total failure, but he's no star either. He could be talented…just not a good fit for *this* position or this company. Both Billy and his company are probably less than thrilled with the arrangement, but they keep on keeping on, often for years and years. What do you think are the composite costs connected to that hiring mistake?

It's no surprise that one of the most important components of the hiring and selection process is the job interview. In our experience, **poor listening during the interview is one of the main culprits of poor selection.**

Most interviewers dig only two or three levels deep into one subject or concern before moving on to the next area of questioning. Their interviews are well-scripted and have an agenda that drives the amount of time that can be spent on any one subject.

Instead, we recommend that the agenda morph into a *conversation* at some point in the interview process. A conversation is more relaxed, and not driven by any agenda or clock. It puts the

---

2   Adrienne Fox, "Drive Turnover Down: Data reveal causes and patterns that help you enhance retention", Vol. 57, No. 7, July 1, 2012, www.shrm.org.

candidate at ease so they can open up and do more of the talking. The use of vertical questioning in such an environment will be much more effective in uncovering whether the candidate is a good fit for the position.

Here is an interview approach you may want to try before a selection is made.

- **Identify a couple of issues that are critical for this position's success.**

- **Develop a good open-ended question to initiate the conversation.**

- **Force yourself to go vertical for at least six levels and even as many as 12 levels on those critical issues!**

Here's Another Story from Jon

I was heading up a project to design and deliver a leadership development program for a company located in Houston, Texas. Because I live in Southern California, I was eager to find a resource in the Houston area who could handle the ongoing delivery of our program once it was established. I asked our recruiters in Houston to line up three finalists who possessed the gravitas of a leadership expert. I explained that the chosen candidate would be training the company's business leaders (who would travel in from all over the country) as well as all those with responsibility for managing others. We needed someone who could lead an interactive two-day session and be able to field questions from bright, assertive participants.

Our recruiters told me that the first candidate I would be interviewing was the strongest. I read the resume in detail and could see why they liked this applicant.

*Because this candidate had already been screened and was being recommended, I prepared to have a **conversation**. This is how the conversation progressed:*

Jon:	"What about this assignment interests you?"
Candidate:	*"I have done a lot of leadership training and thought there was real potential in this."*
Jon:	"What sort of potential did you see?"
Candidate:	*"This could eventually become a virtual learning experience."*
Jon:	"What do you mean by virtual learning?"
Candidate:	*"By virtual I mean a series of online modules."*
Jon:	"What experience do you have with online learning?"
Candidate:	*"I've designed a number of programs."*
Jon:	"What do you enjoy about designing online programs?"

Most hiring managers would have redirected this candidate. They would have reminded them that the assignment called for live delivery, and that online training was not planned.

Any candidate would pick up on that message and be sure to tailor their responses to what the interviewer wanted to hear. Remember, most candidates are looking for a job and want to get an offer.

Instead, Jon wanted the candidate to express their true passion, so he went vertical. He needed to discover what they really liked to do, and what made them prefer online learning to live delivery. Did their particular passion match the requirements of this job?

In the end, a different candidate was chosen and they went on to deliver the program successfully for many years.

Vertical questions help dig deep to reveal what someone truly likes, what they value, and how they approach challenges. You can even uncover how they lead, how they manage, and how they think. Here are a few useful open-ended questions to use in an interview that could lead to some great vertical questions:

- **What responsibility did you have for that decision?**

- **What did you enjoy about that assignment?**

- **What would you have done differently?**

- **What decision that you made changed the outcome in that situation?**

- **What did you gain from that experience?**

By listening and then asking open-ended vertical questions, you can more easily get to the heart of the candidate's passions and experience. Armed with this knowledge, you can best determine their fit for the position in the organization.

Here's a Story from Alexandra

I was being considered for a job where building relationships was considered a critical competency. The company defined this as "developing and using collaborative relationships to facilitate the accomplishment of work goals."

Notice here how the interviewer used open-ended, vertical questions to learn if I possessed this critical skill.

Interviewer: *Tell me about a time when you had to build collaborative relationships to accomplish a work goal?*

Alexandra: I was brought into the HR organization of a global pharmaceutical company to centralize and head the Talent & Leadership Development function. There was very little consistency in the programs being executed to develop talent. And what was being implemented was of poor quality. Historically, people were invested in protecting their turf. No one was working together.

Interviewer: *What did you do to get them to work together?*

Alexandra: I knew it would be impossible to get anything done and sustain it without support from within the businesses. I knew I had to build allies.

I think the first thing I did was to meet with the heads of Training within each business unit. We reviewed what they were doing with their teams, what was working, what wasn't, and what they were passionate about. We discussed roles and responsibilities and how we could work together.

Interviewer: *What reaction did you get from the heads of training?*

Alexandra: I think people were surprised by how willing I was to listen to them, and how eager I was to work with them.

Interviewer: *What convinced them that you were listening?*

Alexandra: After initially building individual relationships, I got all the main stakeholders together as a taskforce. We created a vision, strategy, and goals for our work together. We decided that our first action would be an organizational assessment that would unite the various businesses in our leadership development strategy.

Interviewer: *What was the result of this assessment?*

Alexandra: There were really two outcomes; first, collaboration among those responsible for training increased and second, we created a thoughtful leadership development strategy that was approved by the executive team.

There were multiple touch points in this process. We collaborated every step of the way.

Interviewer: *In what way did the company or the organization benefit from this outcome?*

Alexandra: The work was so much easier because we had so many champions across the organization invested in its success. It was a united effort—the first of its kind for this company.

Interviewer: *What did you enjoy most about building strong working relationships in this example you shared?*

Alexandra: It was rewarding for me to see the organization unite on a strategy to build better leadership talent. I knew that in working together, we could impact the business much more powerfully.

I also value the friendships that developed. I am convinced that our strategy was a better one because of the passion and creativity that came from people working together.

Interviewer: *Thank you for sharing your example.*

The interviewer used six open-ended "What" questions to better understand Alexandra's experience and competency. Almost all of those questions were fully vertical, as they were derived directly from something Alexandra said. As a result, we also learn more about her motivations, her values, and what was gained from the experience.

Hiring good employees is all about listening. It's that simple. Just focus on asking **good questions** to learn how a candidate fulfills your critical success factors (skills, experiences, behaviors, and knowledge). Ask open-ended, vertical, and unbiased "What" questions to identify if your candidate is the best fit.

Try completing these exercises below to help hone your listening skills for the hiring process.

SKILL-BUILDING EXERCISES

1. **Determine Your Needs.** The goal of this exercise is **to improve your listening skills by asking better interview questions.**

   - Think of a job in your area that is currently open. If you have no openings, think of a critical position where preparing before turnover occurs would be a smart move on your part.

   - Make a list of three to five key critical skills (competencies, knowledge, behaviors, or experiences) that the ideal candidate will possess for this position and create simple definitions for each skill.

   - Now develop a list of questions to ask during the interview for each critical skill. Do your best to create about four opening questions for each critical skill. Remember, you want to go *at least six levels deep* after asking your opening question. (Don't forget to use open-ended, vertical questions that begin with "What" as much as possible.)

_____

_____

_____

_____

_____

_____

_____

_____

2. **The Next Best Question.** The goal of this exercise is to help you identify the next best question to ask in an interview setting. Below are some opening questions and candidate responses. Fill in the third column with a vertical question that will help gather more relevant information about the candidate's skills, experience, competency, motivations, etc.

Example

OPENING QUESTION	CANDIDATE RESPONSE	VERTICAL QUESTION
What criteria have you used when considering a difficult decision?	*I think the key is to analyze, but avoid over-examining.*	What do you mean by over-examining? What example can you give me?

Complete the below chart with one or two appropriate follow-up vertical questions.

OPENING QUESTION	CANDIDATE RESPONSE	YOUR VERTICAL QUESTION(S)
Tell me about a time when you had to communicate a difficult message to an employee?	*I recently had to lay off half my team.*	
Share an example of how you overcame a difficult working relationship (with a colleague, client, boss, etc.).	*I was partnered with a teammate on a recent project. Our job was to create a new marketing plan for our client. When it was obvious we had different ideas about how to accomplish the work, I suggested we sit down and talk honestly about our working relationship and the project requirements.*	
What was the result of your decision to move and combine offices?	*We calculated a savings of over $200K by combining our two offices. And we have gained quite a bit of synergy having everyone now co-located.*	

See our sample answers below...

OPENING QUESTION	CANDIDATE RESPONSE	VERTICAL QUESTION
Tell me about a time when you had to communicate a difficult message to an employee?	*I recently had to lay off half my team.*	What were your considerations in communicating this message? What was most important to you as you communicated this message? What did the conversation look like? What was most difficult for you as you communicated this message?
Share an example of how you overcame a difficult working relationship (with a colleague, client, boss, etc.).	*I was partnered with a teammate on a recent project. Our job was to create a new marketing plan for our client.* *When it was obvious we had different ideas about how to accomplish the work, I suggested we sit down and talk honestly about our working relationship and the project requirements.*	What was the outcome of your approach or conversation? What did it look like to facilitate this dialogue with your coworker? What shifts did you make personally? What was the benefit of your decisions to the client or team over time?

OPENING QUESTION	CANDIDATE RESPONSE	VERTICAL QUESTION
What was the result of your decision to move and combine offices?	*We calculated a savings of over $200K by combining our two offices. And we have gained quite a bit of synergy having everyone now co-located.*	What did it take to merge the two teams together effectively? What was your role in the transition? What were your concerns as you made the transition, and how did you handle them?

3. **Go Vertical, Not Horizontal.** The goal of this exercise is to help you practice going vertical with interview questions.

Scenario: You are the hiring executive. The candidate is applying for a management role on your team and will be responsible for integrating a new business into your organization. You need to assess their ability and passion to lead this type of change effectively.

Directions: Read the sample interview questions and responses below, and choose the best follow-up question for each response.

Interview Question Set #1: *(Best answer for each question will follow exercise #4.)*

You: What was your role in driving the change to merge Sport Brands with Swimsuits?

Candidate: *I was the President of Sport Brands. A percentage of our growth strategy called for the acquisition of new brands. We looked at numerous acquisition targets and Swimsuits was the best fit for our goals. Through that merger we went from 5% growth to 15% growth overall.*

You: a.   Tell me more about what you did to lead or drive that acquisition?

b.   How did you go about the analysis?

c.   Who was on your team?

Interview Question Set #2

You: Tell me more about what you did to lead or drive that acquisition?

Candidate: *I set up a Project Swimsuit taskforce comprised of the leaders of all our key functions. We met weekly and each leader played a key role in making the transition from acquisition to integration seamless.*

You: a.   What was the timing?

b.   Walk me through what it looked like during a typical project taskforce meeting? What was a typical agenda, for instance?

c.   What was most challenging for you throughout the change process? What was easiest?

4. **Self-Reflection.** The goal of this exercise is to think about your own experience during your last interview. How effective was the interviewer at asking open-ended, vertical, and "What" questions. What was the impact?

_____

_____

_____

_____

_____

_____

_____

Based on this experience, what do you need to focus on in order to ask better open-ended, vertical and "what" questions during your next hiring or interview process?

_____

_____

_____

_____

_____

_____

_____

_____

_____

_____

_____

_____

_____

_____

_____

_____

_____

_____

_____

_____

_____

_____

_____

Answers for Exercise 3

Question Set #1   *(Best Answer: A)*

Question set #2   *(Best answer: C)*

13

Onboarding

We received a desperate call from a CEO. He was about to hire a Senior Vice President and was feeling gun-shy about the situation. In the last three years, the CEO had filled that position with two different people, but both had failed to fit in. His question? "How do I make sure that this one works out?"

We asked him what he had done previously to bring those two SVP's on board. He said, "Well, talented people don't want anyone micro-managing them, so I hire the best I can find, stand back, and get out of their way."

Unfortunately, many senior executives subscribe to the above onboarding philosophy. While it can work in some situations, it often fails—and fails badly. Yes, most leaders will arrange a couple of meetings so the new hire can get some initial time with their boss and meet their new peers and other key personnel. But that's usually where it ends.

According to the Society for Human Resource Management (SHRM), over half of senior outside hires fail within the first 18 months.[1] SHRM defines onboarding as "helping new hires adjust to the social and performance aspects of their jobs so they can quickly become productive, contributing members of the organization."

We think the problem lies in that "get out of the way" onboarding approach that our desperate CEO regularly employed. It suggests a misunderstanding between two important words; **trust** and **faith**.

Senior executives want to demonstrate that they **trust** the individual they have just selected, so they give them more independence than they should. We say more independence *than they should* because they are mistakenly operating on **faith** rather than **trust**.

KEY THOUGHT

Trust is based on observable behavior. Faith is a belief that does not require observable proof.

If you act as if you trust *without making observations*, then you are actually operating on faith. Faith has a place in our lives, but not when it comes to successfully assimilating a new hire into an organization. Onboarding should not be left to chance.

To trust someone, you need to watch how they behave and how they respond to circumstances that arise. You have to learn how they think and how they make decisions. **The best way to do that is to spend time observing them in various situations. Then, ask open-ended, vertical questions that begin with the word "What."** This gives you a chance to determine whether their approach is acceptable. If it isn't, you can take that opportunity to initiate a dialog that will steer them in a

---

1   Talya N. Bauer, Ph.D., "Onboarding New Employees: Maximizing Success," SHRM Foundation's Effective Practice Guidelines Series, 2010.

successful direction. **Creating opportunities to listen facilitates and accelerates assimilation.**

Onboarding failures are often a result of the assimilation *process*—not the *lack of talent in the selected individual.* Your new hire has likely been successful before and may be successful again. But they have been left to dig a hole for themselves, and it's the hiring executive who should take most of the blame.

Listen in on this sample conversation between an executive (Lauren) and a new direct report:

Lauren: "What are your thoughts about yesterday's project meeting?"

Newbie: *"I thought we could have made more progress."*

Lauren: "What do you think stood in the way?"

Newbie: *"I thought the design team was holding back."*

Lauren: "What do think the reason is that they might do that?"

Newbie: *"I'm not sure."*

Lauren: "May I share some history with you that could explain it?"

If this conversation hadn't occurred, our Newbie would be struggling with a feeling of limited progress and no background information to put it in context. Because Lauren, our wise executive, *listened* (through the use of good questions), and then *transitioned* to sharing a helpful history, the new employee now has a chance of making this team more successful.

Once you have landed your star candidate, it's incumbent upon you to provide them with a smooth transition into their new role. Help them to become a successful member of your team and the organization. The first few months are vital for harnessing a new employee's enthusiasm, so engage their passion and creativity and help them blossom. Listening and asking good questions are the key accelerants in the assimilation process.

A Story from Alexandra

While I was running the Learning & Development team for a major global retailer, one of our large global initiatives was to focus on the first 90 days of the new hire experience. When we looked at all the levers we could pull to make a difference in our business, successful assimilation into the company was critical. In some roles, turnover was 100% in the first three months of service. The revolving door was costing the company big money.

Our solution zeroed in on three things: 1) creating an emotional connection and better understanding of the company, 2) the role of the manager and 3) the role of the employee in assimilating successfully.

The result was a dramatic decrease in turnover which saved the company hundreds of millions of dollars.

First, we created the emotional connection through an Orientation experience that helped our employees relate to our culture. We shared the history and evolving story of our business strategy, competitive landscape, customer profiles, and what we expect of employees.

Steps 2 and 3 dealt with teaching both the manager and the assimilating employee to take equal responsibility for the onboarding process.

Like most things in life, success is more likely when one has a goal in mind and a plan of action. It makes sense then, that if you make a plan to do it, you will find opportunities to listen and ask good questions.

To give you a starting point, we've outlined some of the more important questions you should consider when initiating a conversation during the first 90 days. If you are the **Hiring Individual**, the section below pertains to you. If you are the **Assimilating Individual**, skip over to your section (which immediately follows this one) to learn how to ask questions that will help you to successfully assimilate.

For the Hiring Individual

Here are some sample questions to help shape the conversations a Senior Leader should have with the Assimilating Individual in their first 90 days of employment.

PRE-ARRIVAL TO DAY 1

Questions to ask yourself:

- What is important for the new hire to know about the company history, culture, strategy, goals, and objectives?

- What essential resources does the new hire need for them to be successful?

- What do they need from you or the organization to feel excited about joining the company and starting their new role?

- What can you (or others) do to create an emotional connection to the organization for the new hire?

WEEK 1

Questions to ask yourself:

- What strategic imperatives of the organization are relevant to the new hire?

- What best describes this role and its responsibilities for the new employee? What are the specific standards and expectations for this role and this new employee?

- What should the assimilating employee know about the performance review process?

- What should you share about how you prefer to work with your direct reports? What has worked—and not worked—well in the past? (Pet peeves, important personal data to share, work style, etc.)

- What basic resources and useful tools are needed by the new employee?

- What "unwritten" rules or insights do you need to share with your new employee?

MONTH 1

Questions to ask yourself:

- With which key stakeholders should the new hire meet?

- What information should you share about key stakeholders, other teams, and the business culture?

- What is the company's professional development philosophy?

- What key training does the new employee need now?

- What travel will they need to do?

- What meetings or events will support assimilation, socialization, or interactions with team members and direct reports?

- What resources can the new employee look to for support (like HR, Training, Communications, Marketing, Engineering, Accounting, or Sales)?

MONTH 2

Questions to ask the Assimilating Employee:

- What relationships have you developed with key stakeholders?

- What additional support do you need to continue to build the relationships?

- What, if anything, is standing in the way?

- What are your goals at this point?

- What successes have already been realized?

- What challenges are you having with work initiatives?

- What additional support do you need from me ?

MONTH 3

Questions to ask yourself:

- What perception do you have of this individual's performance to date?

- What's working well? What could they be doing better?

Questions to ask the Assimilating Employee:

- What progress has been made on your goals to date?

- What's working well? What's not working well? What can we do to course correct?

- What can I do to better support you?

- What additional resources are needed?

Using these questions, let's take a look at how Mr. Douglas, a Senior Executive, might lead a conversation with the new hire during her first month in the role:

MONTH 1

Mr. Douglas: Thanks again for taking time to meet with me, Susan. As part of your onboarding, I know you've already met with a few of the key executives. What did you learn in your meeting with Henry?

Newbie: *First, thank you for helping to get all of these meetings scheduled prior to my arrival. I think it's going to make a big difference in getting up to speed quicker. I really enjoyed meeting with Henry. He walked me through the overall strategy as presented to the management team. We had the opportunity to explore a couple of areas in depth where our teams cross over and collaborate.*

Mr. Douglas: What specifically did you discuss in terms of collaboration opportunities?

Newbie: *We looked at the Project Sport first. Specifically, we drilled down into the numbers to better understand the marketing forecast and distribution needs. We identified several areas of handoffs from his team to my team where we need to make sure the roles and responsibilities are clarified.*

Mr. Douglas: Yes, that's been a glitch in the past. What are your plans to address it?

Newbie: *Henry and I identified the key people involved in the project. We asked them to present us with a process map to clarify the work, the roles, and the responsibilities. We'll have that* *by end of this week.*

Mr. Douglas: What obstacles do you foresee, if any?

Newbie: *I think the teams are going to be really happy to have their roles clarified. There may be a few changes, but both teams will appreciate it. I've already begun talking individually with each team member and they believe this is an opportunity. I think the key to success will be ensuring that the rollout includes both our teams, and that we keep meeting periodically so all the transitions are smooth.*

Mr. Douglas: What additional support do you need from me?

Newbie: *On this project, I think we are good. However, I'm having some trouble making sense of something Aidan said during our meeting together. I'd like to get a bit more background on how these groups have worked together in the past and the expectations. I want to make sure I'm representing our department correctly the next time we talk.*

Mr. Douglas: Great. Let's talk about that. What about the conversation was unclear to you?

Asking vertical, open-ended, unbiased "What" questions allows Mr. Douglas to gather data on how the Newbie is feeling, and what she is planning. This helps him assess if she is on the right track and making good decisions. All this conversation (a.k.a.— listening) allows the Newbie to openly discuss results from recent meetings, share her plans, and ask questions when she needs to get more information or support. Trust is beginning to be developed and everyone wins here.

We've taken a look at the Hiring Individual's role in the onboarding process. Now let's take a look at the Newbie's role.

For the Assimilating Individual

New teammates, new culture, new office, new ways of doing things…nothing is familiar at first! There are many things that can bury a person who is new to a position, but our coaching has shown that failure often comes from the individual's *own desire to succeed*. The Senior Executive desperately wants to trust their new hire and that new hire desperately wants to be trusted which tempts them to act more independently than they should. They embody the classic beginner—full of enthusiasm but not necessarily high in competence.

We'll usually get a request for help around the 90-day mark. Simon, the Hiring Individual, wants to know if we can coach his new employee, Theresa, because things just aren't working out. Simon feels disappointed in Theresa's work and now his negative opinion is almost impossible to turn around. Simon's timing seems to fit with the findings of Michael Watkins who wrote *The First 90 Days*. In his preface he writes, "Transitions are critical times when small differences in your actions can have a disproportionate impact on results."

What happened? It's likely that the Assimilating Individual made some mistake, and then they are perceived by others as "digging a hole" for themselves. When they become aware of that perception, they start digging harder. The hole eventually gets so deep that the Hiring Executive decides it's too late to salvage this new hire. The situation may lead to termination—or even worse—the *retention* of an individual who has not earned effective status in the organization. Everyone loses!

Why does the Newbie keep digging? Why don't they ask for help?

They probably don't want to give the impression that they are weak or unqualified. They need to prove that they are decisive and can take action.

To prevent this, anyone new to a position needs to take charge of their own assimilation. Their boss may provide significant support (that's great), but they can't rely on that because they still will not be forgiven if anything goes wrong.

You will be more successful in a new position if you ask open-ended questions that are vertical and begin with the word "What." Your curiosity will be admired and you'll be rewarded by an increased understanding of the business and culture that surrounds you. You'll have a better feeling for how your boss makes decisions, what your peers need from you, and how you can assist your reports. You'll be seen as a collaborative, consensual team player. And most importantly, you will be building a **foundation of trust.**

Let's take a look at some great questions to help the Assimilating Individual shape the conversation and grow into their new role during the first few months.

PRE-ARRIVAL TO WEEK 1

Questions to ask yourself:

- What can I do in advance to learn more about the company's history, mission, key business strategies, market perceptions, organizational structure and important policies?

- What is my role and what are my responsibilities?

- What should I expect from the first 60 to 90 days?

- What projects and initiatives will I be working on and what are likely to be the key milestones and dates?

- What are the standards and expectations I should be aware of?

- What input will my boss want to have on my developing goals and plans? What level of independence will I be expected to have?

- What are my goals for the first month and when should I finalize goals for the year?

- What are my team's goals, and how do they fit in with the larger goals of my department, function, business, or company?

- What are the key metrics I will use to measure my team's success?

DURING MONTH 1

NOTE: *Before you ask your boss any question, consider this. Some bosses prefer that you show the initiative to make your own observations and then have them confirm or modify them. Others would rather you ask them questions up front. Determine which of these types your own boss is before proceeding.*

Questions to ask your boss:

- Who are the key stakeholders I need to meet with as I continue to assimilate into my new role?

- What do I need to accomplish during these stakeholder meetings?

- What are the collaboration points and dependencies between my team and a key stakeholder's team?

- What insight, history, or information would be helpful to know as I approach meetings with key stakeholders?

- What are the department's strengths?

- What are my team's strengths and greatest challenges?

- What does it take to be successful in my area?

- May I ask for some additional information about Project X?

Questions to ask each of your direct reports:

- What is their background, work experience, and relevant training?

- What are their career goals?

- How do they like to be managed?

- What is presently working well in the department and on the team?

- What is causing problems and needs to be changed?

- What do they need to know about me?

Questions to ask your team as a group:

NOTE: *When conducting a new leader assimilation meeting, it's helpful to have your Human Resources representative facilitate the meeting while you LISTEN.*

- How does the team function currently?

- What is the team excited about or nervous about?

- Regarding team projects and how they are managed, what is working well and what needs improvement?

- What important projects and initiatives are underway? What support does the team need for these?

- What does the team need to know about you?

DURING MONTHS 2 AND 3

Questions to ask yourself to help shape conversations with your boss, your team, or key stakeholders:

- What challenges am I having with work initiatives?

- What additional support do I need from my boss?

- What support do I need from the key stakeholders?

- What successes have already been realized?

- What are my goals?

Using the questions above as inspiration, let's take a look at how a conversation may progress between Karl, our new hire and Ms. Chen, the Senior Executive.

Karl: "May I ask some questions about yesterday's meeting?"

Ms. Chen: *"Sure."*

Karl: "The project team seemed to be holding back. What can you share with me that might explain that?"

Ms. Chen: *"I think they've been put on the spot before."*

Karl: "What did you observe that I might do differently?"

By using some pointed, opened-ended, vertical questions that began with the word "What," our newbie, Karl, quickly got to the heart of the matter. If Karl is truly open to the feedback he is about to receive, and then acts on it, this newbie will be well on his way to more successful future interactions with the project team and his boss.

We cannot say enough about the potential of asking questions to help you create a more effective onboarding process. The right questions can empower New Hires to craft their own reality at work. And for Hiring Executives, questions help to ensure that their "investment" will pay off.

The following exercises are designed to help you put listening skills and asking questions into practice during your next encounter with onboarding.

SKILL-BUILDING EXERCISES

1. **Questions for the First 90 Days.** The purpose of this exercise is to get you to think about what conversations will make your new hire's assimilation a greater success. For each phase of the onboarding, we want you to think about the kinds of questions you should focus on.

    - **Manager.** Using the 90-day timeline, develop your own list of questions for discussion with your new employee.

    - **Employee.** Using the 90-day timeline, put together a list of the *unanswered questions* that you need to discuss.

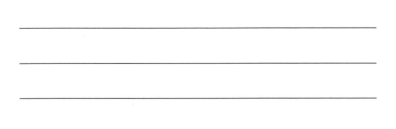

_____

_____

_____

_____

2. **Welcome Meeting from Both Perspectives.** The goal of this exercise is to better understand the conversations you need to be prepared for as a New Employee and as the Hiring Manager during the first week of welcome meetings. The tone of this meeting will help set the stage for future meetings.

    Do **both** the a. and b. exercises, whether you are the Hiring Manager or the Assimilating Employee.

    a. **Manager perspective:** Put together a list of questions for your first meeting with your New Employee (from the perspective of the Manager). What do you still need to ask the Employee? As you talk about work initiatives, key stakeholders, etc.—what can you do to ask open-ended, vertical questions that begin with the word "What?"

    b. **Newbie perspective:** Put together a list of questions for your first meeting with your Manager (from the perspective of the New Employee). What do you still need to ask the Manager? As you talk about work initiatives, key stakeholders, etc.—what can you do to ask open-ended, vertical questions that begin with the word "What?" What support, direction and additional help do you need?

Course Correct. The goal of this exercise is to help you craft a conversation that will support getting you back on track. Again, we'll look at this from the New Employee and the Manager perspective.

Newbie: Imagine you are currently "digging a hole" or noticing that things are not progressing as well as you'd like. Use this list of questions to help you prepare for a conversation with your Manager or the appropriate individual. Consider the following:

- Identify the problem—what do you need help with specifically?

- Write out the situation and your role.

- Write out a series of questions to help you gain support or additional resources. Determine how to begin a conversation about what needs to be fixed, changed, or addressed.

- Write down any burning questions you may have.

- Write down any brilliant ideas you may have.

Hint: *Make sure you use open-ended, vertical, "What" questions. Also, remember how to transition to sharing your opinion, if necessary.*

Manager: Imagine that things are not progressing as well as possible for your New Employee. They are performing below your standards or you are concerned that they are headed in the wrong direction on a particular task. Use the list of questions below to help you prepare for your conversation with them. Consider the following:

- Identify the problem—what do you think needs to be addressed?

- Write out the situation and your expectations of the New Employee's roles and responsibilities.

- Write out a series of questions to help you gain clarity about the Newbie's thinking, their actions, or their inactions to date.

Hint: *Make sure you use open-ended, vertical, "what" questions. Also, don't forget to ask permission to share your opinion when offering counsel or wanting to express your ideas.*

_____

_____

_____

_____

_____

_____

_____

14

Delegating

All leaders need to delegate—it is an important part of managing others. But not every leader knows how to do so. And if you are not employing good listening skills, you will end up frustrated by your results.

When coaching managers, we've noticed that learning to delegate effectively is one of the major hurdles they face as they rise through the ranks. We all experience it. What an important change it is to go from *doing* all the work, to *leading others* as THEY do the work.

We coached an engineering manager who was struggling to make the leap into effective delegation. When we met him, he was so afraid to leave his team on their own, that he found himself working very long hours and, (much to his wife's dismay), never went on vacation.

The client company was eager to see this talented, emerging leader let go of the small stuff and overcome this barrier to promotion. His area of the business was growing rapidly and they needed him to concentrate on the vital matters where his expertise could come into play. He was a good candidate for advancement, but if he wanted to move up, he was going to have to start delegating more.

The problem is, they suspected he didn't know how. Our interviews with the engineering manager confirmed those suspicions.

Coach: What stands in the way of passing off some of your work to other members on your team?

Manager: *They just aren't ready for it.*

Coach: What's your plan to get them ready?

Manager: *I don't have one.*

We continued to ask our "What" questions so that we could understand all of the barriers and opportunities in this situation. It soon became clear that our manager needed to learn the tools of delegating successfully.

We began a coaching program that included our process for effective delegation. Finally, we worked on how we could build the manager's trust of just one person at a time, until that investment led to a thriving independent team.

KEY THOUGHT
There are three important ingredients in effective delegation: clarifying your expectations, knowing the individual's level of competence, and gauging their level of commitment. All are greatly served by asking questions.

To delegate successfully, follow this process:

1. Ask yourself what your **expectations** are.

2. Ask yourself if you deem this person to be **competent** for this task.

3. Ask yourself if they are likely to be **committed** to the task.

4. If yes, then **share** your expectations for the task with the individual.

5. Ask the individual to **articulate their understanding** of your expectations.

6. Ask them to advise you of the **support they'll** need to augment their competence.

7. Ask questions to **gauge** their level of **commitment.**

8. Follow up regularly and ask questions that **measure their progress and success.**

Let's look at each of these steps...

1. Ask yourself what your expectations are.

The most competent of your direct reports may be able to take an unclear assignment and turn it into a success. Chances are, however, that most of your team needs some clarity in the assignment to maximize their performance. If you don't know what you expect from this person at the outset, then you are launching the task inefficiently and risking failure for yourself—and them as well.

Inefficiency arises from the constant monitoring that needs to be done when expectations are unclear or continually shifting. We encourage you to spend more time at the front end when delegating a task so you avoid wasting the time it takes to closely supervise a project midstream.

Failure is not a good outcome, but that's what happens when expectations are ambiguous. While those involved clearly understand they failed to complete the assignment correctly, there is an underpinning of frustration and demotivation created by the lack of clarity surrounding the project. And this reflects back upon the leader.

Here are some questions you can ask yourself:

- **What does the successful outcome of this project look like?**

- **What resources (time, money, human capital) should it take?**

- **What are the key milestones that I want to be aware of?**

- **What boundaries must the participants recognize?**

- **What amount of autonomy can I allow in the scoping and performance of this task?**

We recognize that you may not have the answers to all of these questions. The participants might need to answer some of the questions for themselves.

2.   Ask yourself if you deem this person to be competent for this task.

Consider what degree of skill and experience they have for doing the task at hand. This will determine the *level of direction* you'll need to provide. If they are capable and competent, less management is required. If they don't have the necessary level of competence, you probably need to monitor the task more closely. That means you'll have to give them more specific directions on how to complete the task, provide them with training, or even assign more experienced talent to augment their efforts.

Ask yourself questions like the ones below:

- **What applicable skill, knowledge, or experience does this person have?**

- **What has their performance been in the past?**

- **What degree of independence have they shown on other projects?**

- **How much support or guidance am I able to provide?**

- **What other resources may be required?**

The answers to these questions are influenced by how well you know the individual. The less you know someone, the more time you should expect to spend with them…and the more careful you should be about choosing them to handle this task.

3.   Ask yourself if they are likely to be committed to the task.

Committed employees work more independently, are more productive, inspire others, and spot opportunities that are tangent to the task at hand. The probability of success increases when the assignment is in the hands of those who are committed. Will every project inspire commitment? *No.* Will every individual bring commitment to the project? No. But assessing the possibility of creating commitment is both an obligation and an opportunity in your role as a leader.

Commitment naturally springs from a combination of elements when people:

- **Do the work they enjoy (like an engineer solving a problem or a sales person interacting with a customer).**

- **Work on something meaningful (to society or to the success of the business, for example).**

- **Do something that is both challenging and achievable.**

- **Have an appropriate amount of autonomy for the task.**

Here are some questions you might ask yourself:

- **What does this person seem to enjoy (solving problems, coordinating the efforts of others, working as an individual contributor, etc.)?**

- **What is meaningful about this assignment?**

- **What is it about this project that will make it challenging yet achievable?**

- **What are you willing to do to make sure this project will be successful and thus drive even greater ongoing commitment?**

- **What level of freedom (based on past experience with this person) can you allow on this project?**

4.   Share your expectations for the task.

Use the answers to the questions you have asked yourself to craft a message that clearly defines what you are expecting of this person.

Imagine that you have received a report from your Asian division that a hospital has found major defects with an infusion system used for critically ill patients. This is what the task delegation might sound like when speaking to a seasoned product design engineer who has led problem-solving teams in the past: *"We have received a report that our I30 Infuser is malfunctioning in the largest hospital in Shanghai. I need you to gather all of the information you can on the failure. Then identify a swat team and bring them in for a situation meeting early tomorrow. Please check your calendar. I suspect you'll need to go to China as soon as possible."*

This is what the task delegation might sound like when speaking to a less experienced design engineer who doesn't yet have a track record of leading teams: *"We have received a report that our I30 Infuser is malfunctioning in the largest hospital in Shanghai. I would like you to call our rep in Shanghai and have her send us all of the available information on the failure. Do you have the contact information for that rep? Good. I'd like to have that information available for a meeting I'm calling early tomorrow morning. I will gather a team of people to work on this with us. You should check your calendar. I may want you to go to Shanghai with me."*

5. Ask the individual to articulate their understanding of your expectations.

If you are doing all the talking, how will you know if the employee understands your expectations? You're thinking, "Well, if they don't understand what I want, they'll ask me for clarification, right?" Sounds logical, but maybe ***they think they do understand*** what you want or maybe they're uncomfortable asking you exactly what you mean.

Imagine this Conversation...

Bradford: "Jennifer, please handle this client's concern about the delay on their project's delivery date."

Jennifer: *"Uh, okay."*

Whoa! This is a delegated task headed for disaster. For all that Bradford knows, Jennifer is delighted to take on his task. But if this is his idea of good delegating, he deserves everything he's going to get. Our delegator has no idea when Jennifer will begin to act on the task, how she will go about doing it, or even if she's capable of doing it. And, by the way, *the reality* is that Jennifer has no clue how to allay this client's fears about missing their deadline, but she is uncomfortable admitting that to her boss. When things go wrong—and they will—Bradford will be quick to penalize Jennifer for lack of compliance. But it is *he* who is the cause of this problem.

When you delegate a task to someone else, be sure to have them put your expectations into *their own words*. You need to know that they understand the final result you want them to deliver.

Some leaders leave this step out. They fear that it will signal a lack of trust. We believe securing clarity is worth the minor risk of offending the employee. In fact, we've found that most people appreciate the extra care that their leader takes in seeking alignment.

Why wait until you are dissatisfied with the wrong result? Why not use questions to confirm what the employee plans to do to meet your standards of execution?

Here are some questions you might ask them:

- **I want to be sure we are aligned on the details of this project. What do you see as the key expectations for this assignment?**

- **I hope that I have shared enough about this assignment. Sometimes it helps me to hear the message back so that I'm sure I've covered everything. What would you say to describe the task I've asked you to take on?**

6.   Ask what support they need to augment their competence.

You may have decided in Step Number 3, (where you ask yourself if you deem this person competent), that the individual has some blind spots that need to be accommodated. It would be ideal if they recognized that fact on their own and requested assistance. But they may not be ready to do that in this first meeting. You might need to let them think about this question and return later with an answer.

If they do not identify a need but you believe the need exists, use the following questions to raise the subject in a way that lessens the possibility of demotivating this individual.

Here are some questions you can ask:

- **What support is needed for you to be successful with this assignment?**

- **What can I do to help you be successful with this project?**

- **You said you don't see a need for any support on this project. May I ask you that question again after you've had a chance to sleep on it?**

- **You have said you don't need any support on this project. May I share some of my thoughts with you?**

- **You said that you have what you need to successfully complete this project. May I share what I see as some opportunities for you to ensure your success?**

Notice that we are asking for permission to share our ideas.

7.   Ask questions that gauge their commitment.

You have already thought about the possibility that they may or may not be motivated to work on this assignment. Now is the time for a meeting to get that subject out on the table so you can leverage something positive or overcome a potential negative.

One Way to Test Commitment:

- **Is the individual paralyzed by the prospect of getting a new assignment?**

- **Or are they quickly moving forward to the planning stage?**

The time it takes an individual to go through this transition will depend on the size of the task and their personality. In this meeting, or soon after, you want to hear your employee saying something like, *"I have an idea of how to get this started,"* or, *"Now that I've thought about it, I could use an extra software engineer on the team,"* or, *"I said I could get this done by the end of the quarter but we need to discuss what that would mean to this other project."*

All of these comments sound different than, *"I haven't had a chance to work out a project plan yet,"* or *"I'm still concerned about leaving that other team on their own while I work on this."* Sentences like these could be the chant of a perennial worrier. But they might also be a sign of someone who has not yet committed to the new assignment.

Here are some questions you might ask to test their commitment:

- **What timeframe do you need to put together a preliminary project plan and bring back any questions we should address?**

- **What concerns do you have about this assignment now that you have the whole story?**

- **What do you see as the first step you'll need to take to get going?**

- **Yesterday, you seemed concerned about your current project load. We talked about you planning to make some adjustments. What ideas have you come up with?**

8.   Follow up regularly and ask questions to measure success.

Open-ended, vertical questions are the surest way to find out what is really going on in a project. By now, you have identified the major milestones for follow-up and determined the frequency of these checkpoints based on your experience with the individual.

Here are some questions you might ask to measure the status of the task's success:

- **This project has fallen behind. What actions are being taken to get it back on schedule?**

- **Some issues have surfaced. What resources do you require in order to solve them?**

- **This project is on schedule. What are the key actions that have contributed to this success?**

Putting delegation into practice

Understanding the dynamics of delegation is crucial to your success. It can prevent you from under or over-supervising someone on a particular task. If you have ever felt micromanaged —or equally awful—left alone on the sidelines, you know how demotivating and frustrating it can be.

Let's zero in on some delegation conversations for various situations.

SITUATION   Competent employee who lacks confidence doing this specific project.

Delegator: "How are you feeling about handling the proposal for The Fictitious Company?

Brendan: *"Good. I'm going to talk with Marketing and make sure the proposal is buttoned up by the end of the week. We are running the numbers portion right now. I plan to follow up with the client directly today to let them know our timing, and again on Friday with the final proposal."*

Delegator: "Sounds like you have a great plan in place. I'm glad you are going to talk to Marketing. What concerns do you have?

Brendan: *"I'm a little concerned about the final format. I've done a lot of proposals for other clients, but I'm still unsure of The*

> *Fictitious Company's standards. Do you have any past examples of what was submitted and well-received by them?"*

Delegator: "May I share a concern about that?"

Brendan: *"Yes."*

Delegator: "We have a tremendous opportunity next year with this client. I asked you to do this project for a reason. The level of work we've submitted in the past for The Fictitious Company is no longer good enough. I think what you have done with XYZ Corporation represents the standard we should now follow. You've done great work before and I have confidence that you'll do the same here."

Brendan: *"That's really helpful, thank you!"*

Delegator: "Since we are going to change things up, would you be willing to share a draft with me before we submit it to the client?"

Brendan: *"Yes. I'll get the draft to you by Wednesday. If you can get me your edits by Thursday, we will be good to go with the final on Friday."*

In the conversation above, our Delegator used all the characteristics of asking good questions. They also tailored how much clarity was needed based on Brendan's competence and commitment.

Notice that the Delegator's last question highlights an area of concern ("Since we are going to change things up..."). This prompted them to pull the delegation back a little by asking to see a draft. Delegating is often a fluid situation.

Now, let's imagine this same conversation with someone who has little competence and lots of commitment. Our Delegator needs to provide much more direction, support, and clarity of expectations. Let's take a look at this conversation and how different it sounds:

SITUATION   **Employee has low competence but loads of commitment.**

Delegator: "What are you feeling about handling The Fictitious Company's questions?

Rachel: *"I'm really excited about the challenge, but honestly I'm not quite sure where to begin."*

Delegator: "What can I help you with specifically?

Rachel: *"I'd love to walk through a project plan with you if that's ok?"*

Delegator: "Great, let's schedule an hour for this afternoon and we can go step-by-step through what needs to happen— everything from what Marketing can do, to when you'll follow up with the client, and what the final proposal should look like."

Rachel: *"That would be really helpful. I want to make sure I not only meet, but surpass your expectations!"*

Delegator: "We have a tremendous opportunity next year with this client. I think the work you have done with XYZ Corporation is really going to help you with this client. I know this is new for you, but I'm confident that once we walk through it together you'll learn fast."

Rachel: *"It's nice to hear you say that!"*

Delegator: "Great, I'll see you this afternoon. After we go through the project plan, we'll calendar some subsequent meetings to discuss the project's status through completion. In the meantime, please get together a couple of sample proposals we've submitted to XYZ Corporation and ask Darcy for a copy of the project plan she used with UVW, Inc."

Rachel: *"Okay, I'll do both of those things and see you this afternoon. Thanks again!"*

SKILL-BUILDING EXERCISES

1. **Delegate it.** The goal of this exercise is to practice using questions for preparation in delegating an assignment. Think about a real-life project that you need to delegate and use the space in this chart to answer questions.

QUESTION	WRITE YOUR THOUGHTS HERE....
1. Describe the assignment you are delegating. What are your expectations?	Creating and delivering the sales pitch for new client acquisition.
2. Is the person competent for the task?	Yes, highly competent. Successfully executed multiple sales presentations for strategic client acquisition meetings.
3. Are they likely to be committed to the task?	Yes, they like being in front of clients. They are eligible for incentive compensation and end-of-year sales bonus.

QUESTION	WRITE YOUR THOUGHTS HERE....
4. Are they able to articulate your expectations?	Yes. They clearly understand my directions and concerns.
5. What support do they need to augment their competence?	Need one staff analyst to help build the presentation and run analytics.
6. What will you do to measure success and progress?	Successful client acquisition.

Your idea here

QUESTION	WRITE YOUR THOUGHTS HERE....
1. Describe the assignment you are delegating. What are your expectations?	
2. Is the person competent for the task?	
3. Are they likely to be committed to the task?	
4. Are they able to articulate your expectations?	

QUESTION	WRITE YOUR THOUGHTS HERE....
5. What support do they need to augment their competence?	
6. What will you do to measure success and progress?	

2. **Self-Reflection.** The purpose of this exercise is to help you identify where you need to spend more time asking good questions in your delegation efforts. Think about a recent assignment you delegated that didn't go as well as you would have liked. Use the steps outlined in the chapter to identify where you went wrong. Then think about what you could have done differently to change the outcome.

_____

_____

_____

_____

_____

_____

15

Coaching

Our roots in coaching run deep.

We coach leaders at the top of organizations, mid-level leaders who need to hone their skills in anticipation of their next big role, and leaders who risk plateauing if they don't repair a behavior. We help teams that struggle to hit their stride as well as teams that are humming along towards their next major goal. Regardless of the assignment, every successful coaching conversation relies heavily on good listening skills, and that, as you now know, is all about asking the next great question.

Recently we were asked to coach a leader as he transitioned to Chief Executive Officer after successfully running a portion of the business. His transition included acclimating to the new role, moving to another state, and leading a team of his former peers, while simultaneously heading up several high-value acquisitions. As you can imagine, we had lots to talk about!

At the end of each coaching session, he would comment that

the most valuable part of the coaching was the space we created by asking him questions. "Your persistence in asking questions that were multiple levels deep always drove my thought process further. Ultimately, I'd find the answers I never knew I had."

What is Your Role at this Moment?

Questions are often the best place to start when you realize someone needs your coaching skills. But you may want to direct your questions inward at first to determine what role you should be playing. Is it really to be a coach or might it be something else?

There are potentially four hats you can wear—that of the:

- **Leader**

- **Mentor**

- **Coach**

- **Counselor**

While there is overlap in some of these roles, you'll want to slightly alter your conduct for each one. And depending on which part you are playing, you might get a different outcome. Keep in mind that some of these roles are appropriate to a business situation, but one of them seldom is.

Let's take a quick look at the differences.

Leader   *One who leads, commands, guides, and directs.*

Mentor   *A wise and trusted teacher, guide, and friend.*

Coach   *Someone who provides a process to identify and overcome barriers to effectiveness. A coach will support and encourage the coachee to reach an important goal.*

Counselor *Someone who provides a process to identify and work through personal problems.*

So which role is often inappropriate in a business context?

Correct! Chances are you are not equipped to be a counselor (unless you have a degree you didn't tell us about). Playing the role of counselor or therapist could change the relationship drastically. Instead, you should guide the individual towards resources to help them explore any personal problems.

So that leaves three roles that you could play: The Leader, The Mentor, and The Coach. You should be able to move somewhat seamlessly between these roles.

If the situation requires that you play the role of The Leader, then we hope by now that we've clearly justified the benefits of your using open-ended, vertical questions that begin with the word "What." Additionally, you'll find that all the application chapters *(found in Part III)* will help you to use great questions as a leader. So, for this chapter, let's further narrow the field to the roles of The Coach and The Mentor.

Let's focus our attention even further. Although Coaching and Mentoring are made from the same cloth, Mentoring is usually more focused on *subject matter* than *behavior*. Consequently, if you were mentoring your employee, you might place a stronger emphasis on *"telling"* them about a subject than *"asking"* them about a behavior.

Because Coaching is often focused on behaviors, it is much more dependent on the *What You Don't Know About Listening* approach to asking questions. Therefore, Coaching will be the focus of this chapter. (After all, it IS the title of the chapter!)

Coaching is a unique and powerful process. When you are coaching, your total focus is on supporting and encouraging someone to make important changes or to achieve a specific goal. This requires you to listen to the individual's words and *what's behind them.* You must hold your coachee accountable and demand they tell you the truth. Above all, you are committed to their success. Amazingly, all of this is possible when you ask powerful questions, become curious, and listen.

The Coaching Process

Most professional coaches have a process that describes the stages of engagement with a client. As a leader, you may want that same awareness of where you are in the coaching process when working with an employee.

There are essentially four phases to a successful coaching process.

1. **Intention**
2. **Information**
3. **Instruction**
4. **Internalization**

Let's take a look at each one.

Intention

Before you begin, you'll need to be clear about what you want to achieve. In other words, what is the purpose of this coaching? Both the leader and coachee should be clear about the intention of this work. Sometimes we call this "designing the alliance". The idea here is that you want to be deliberate in your work rather than operating by default. You need a clear understanding of what you are trying to accomplish. Here are some great questions that the coach should ask:

- **What is the reason for this coaching?**
    - » To improve unacceptable performance?
    - » To enhance current performance?
    - » To prepare for a challenging assignment?
    - » To strengthen succession readiness?
    - » To explore career options?
    - » To motivate?
    - » To reach an important goal or result?
    - » To make or create an important change?

- **What can we do to prioritize the needs?**
- **What is the outcome we desire from this coaching?**

Here's how this conversation might sound:

Coach   What is the purpose of our coaching together?

Employee   *"I want to improve my presentation skills, increase my chances for advancement, and enhance my skills as a project leader."*

Coach   Which of these is most important to you at the moment?

Employee   *"Well, there's a national sales meeting coming up and I'm scheduled to make a presentation."*

Coach   So, if we work on presentation skills, what is your desired outcome?

Employee   *"I want to feel prepared and comfortable giving speeches in front of the sales team. And I want to have good quality material to deliver."*

By using quality questions and listening, the coach can help the employee articulate and prioritize their specific need for the coaching. Once that is decided, they can agree on what a successful outcome might look like.

Information

From the information you've discovered in the Intention phase, you might think you know what to do, but it's a good idea to collect additional information to confirm that you're headed in the right direction. After a bit of diagnosis, you might find you need to revise the intention of the coaching. Here are some questions to ask:

- **What data is available to confirm that the right need is being addressed?**
  - » What sort of assessment might be conducted to confirm a cause-and-effect relationship that can be addressed?
  - » What specific behaviors or skill deficits contribute to the identified need?
  - » What are others observing?
  - » What additional information do you need in order to achieve a successful outcome?

Instruction

Different people learn in different ways. And different situations might require different interventions. **Instruction** suggests leader-directed teaching.

Nowadays, teaching includes a wide array of delivery methods. We use the term "instruction" in its broadest form. It may mean actual *training* or it could mean *quality coaching conversations or experiences* that lead the coachee to important self-discovery and insight. Here are some questions to ask:

- What type of training, skill development, or coaching is needed?

- In what way does this person learn most successfully? Do they like to read, experience, or witness information?

- What resources are available to help them learn in their preferred way?

- Which delivery method is best in this situation?

Internalization

Coaching has little impact if the learning is not sustained. Leaders that coach look for the opportunity to support learners in a way that pays dividends for the long term. Learners need to internalize the experience so that the new skills and behaviors become second nature to them. Here are some questions to ask:

- What will help this person sustain the change?

- What can I do to periodically audit whether the coachee has maintained a beneficial change?

- What follow-up assessment should the coachee consider in order to confirm their learning has been successful?

- What are others observing about the individual's perceived changes?

Incorporating the four phases—Intent, Information, Instruction and Internalization—can help you create a successful environment for learning.

We've made our discussion of process quite brief. Our emphasis in *What You Don't Know About Listening* is more on the conversation.

KEY THOUGHT

It's the conversation that is at the center of coaching. And it is the asking rather than the telling throughout the coaching process that creates the best learning.

Though coaching is more about asking than telling, it's sometimes acceptable for the coach to share an opinion. Revisit Chapter 8 where we cover how to ask permission to do so.

A Story from Jon

Some of you may think the following is coming from outside a business context, but it's not. For a coach, the approach would be very good for business!

Recently, my wife and I spent a week at a resort in Arizona. It was our third visit there and I had come to really enjoy the golf instruction they offered.

After lunch one day, I hurried to the practice center in hopes of catching part of a group lesson. To my surprise, I was the only guest to show up—a rare incident.

The head pro offered me a one-on-one session and I leapt at the chance. I asked what club he wanted me to use and he said, "Let's just sit down over here."

We sat in the lounge area of the golf center for nearly half an hour before we ever touched a piece of equipment. When we did get a piece of equipment, it was a tennis racquet (but that's another story).

This pro knew that the key to great coaching is to ask the next great question. This is how our session started.

Pro   What are your goals when it comes to golf?
            (Intention)

Jon   *I would like to play consistently in the 80's.*

Pro   What can you tell me about your golf game?
            (Information)

Jon   *I play once or twice a week. Sometimes I might go a month or two without playing.*

Pro   How often do you practice?
            (Information)

Jon   *Occasionally. I like to play more than practice.*

Pro   What do you think it will take to accomplish your goal?
            (Instruction)

Jon   *I can tell from your line of questioning that it will probably take more practice and more playing.*

Pro   I think that is right. Are you willing to do that?
            (Internalization)

Jon   *I'm not sure I'm ready to give up my other passions and dedicate that much time to golf.*

Pro   Given that, what can you do to enjoy the game of golf more?
            (He returns to Intention)

Do you see how the Pro brought me to the edge of a conclusion that I needed to arrive at on my own? The only way for me enjoy golf is to take pressure off myself about my score. Unless I was willing to invest in improving my game, I was only going to frustrate myself.

Coaching is Asking the Next Great Question

Even though we practice asking questions in the work we do, it is eye opening when it's used on us! Encouraging someone to reflect inwardly is stimulating and important in helping them to come to a decision on their own. Time and time again we see that self-realization is more effective than simply being told. Asking questions creates the space for powerful self-learning.

Coaching is Also *More* Than Asking the Next Great Question

The next great question in coaching often comes by paying heed to your intuition, listening *beyond the words*, and trusting where your gut takes you. This means you have to observe the body language of your client, take in the surroundings, and *feel the air* in the room.

A Word of Warning

Many "novice" listeners see themselves as more advanced than they really are and take the suggestion to use their intuition as an invitation to skip much of what we are trying to teach. Slow down. Master your listening skills first.

To Be Successful, Coaching Must Be an Active Collaboration

Coaching requires *active collaboration* on the part of the coach and the client. The coach's job is to ask good questions that help drive the individual's self-discovery and learning. These questions should stem from the knowledge that the coachee is capable, creative, and resourceful. The coachee's job is to be willing to answer all questions truthfully and do the necessary work.

Coaching Needs to be Ongoing

Many times leaders are reluctant to coach until formal opportunities arise, such as performance reviews. We believe this does a disservice to the leader, the individual, and the organization.

Coaching to enhance someone's performance should happen whenever the need arises. And it should be an ongoing conversation, not an annual event. Performance reviews are not a substitute for coaching and in fact, they could have the *opposite effect* if that's the only time that the leader ever meets to talk about performance.

We admire the work of Beverly Kaye and Julie Winkle Giulioni. In their book, *Help Them Grow or Watch Them Go*, they say:

"...less is more. An interaction doesn't have to have a minimum threshold to count as a conversation. You don't get more points for length. You get more points for stimulating thinking. Would you rather sit down with an employee for two hours and map out a career plan for the year or do the same thing in a dozen ten-minute conversations over the year?"

We agree with Kaye and Giulioni that multiple ten-minute conversations would effectively stimulate more thinking. And that means more creativity, more collaboration, more understanding, and more self-realization. Make your coaching an ongoing endeavor. If you don't, you're sure to end up with a resentful and less engaged employee who'll be wondering why you bothered to bring up the topic at all if you weren't willing to continue to listen to them, support them, and create an ongoing conversation.

Imagine the coach of a college basketball team waiting until the very end of the season to share their thoughts about how the star center for the team played in the *first* game of the season. That coach would be a goner! Basketball coaching happens in the moment, constantly shouted from the sideline as the players race from one end of the court to the other. To make a successful team, you should offer your "players" the same support.

A Story from Alexandra

In one of my earlier jobs, I managed a corporate Learning and Development team. Lucky for me I had a phenomenal boss who modeled coaching beautifully and encouraged me to use those skills with my team. My boss and I met weekly in one-on-one conversations. During these meetings we discussed business projects, updates, and timelines, among other issues. There was also time for her to give me feedback on my performance.

Our quarterly "informal" performance reviews flowed seamlessly from those weekly meetings and then all the conversations streamed into my yearly performance review. Although it may seem redundant, it never felt that way. Rather, it felt like a continuous conversation that we were able to build upon. This process made it easy for my boss to discuss appropriate "stretch assignments" and to convey that my talents were recognized.

I used this same coaching structure with my own team and it worked perfectly. There were no surprises. If something needed course correcting, we addressed it in the moment. We were a highly efficient, productive, and collaborative team and I am certain that a huge contributor to our success was having a structure for these ongoing dialogs or coaching conversations.

You don't have to have a "coaching culture" to start coaching your employees. You just need to be willing to begin the conversation, start listening and asking some good questions! If this is new for you, be transparent with your actions. Maybe you want to ask your employees for permission to begin doing some formal coaching together. If they agree, be open to receiving their feedback on what's working and not working. Coaching should be an active collaboration.

You can use the exercises below to sharpen some of your coaching skills before you begin.

SKILL-BUILDING EXERCISES

1. **Great Coaches.** Part of becoming a great coach, is having a clear picture of the end result. Think about a great coach you have experienced or someone who exemplifies the characteristics you want to emulate. Use the questions below to help you get clear about what is important to you as a coach.

   a. What characteristics stand out to you about great coaches?

   b. How prepared are they as coaches? How did they prepare?

   c. What do they convey?

   d. What characteristics specifically do you want to emulate?

   e. What's important to you in a coaching relationship?

   _____

   _____

   _____

2. **The Next Great Question.** The purpose of this exercise is to help you become more fluid in asking the next great question—a key skill of a great coach. Use the sample scenarios below to come up with the next great coaching question(s).

Sample Business Cases

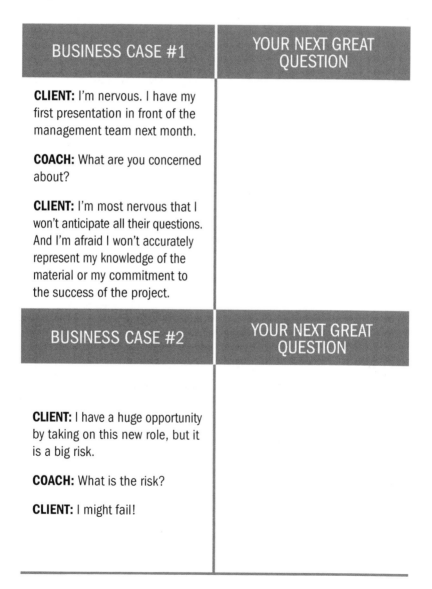

BUSINESS CASE #1	YOUR NEXT GREAT QUESTION
CLIENT: I'm nervous. I have my first presentation in front of the management team next month. **COACH:** What are you concerned about? **CLIENT:** I'm most nervous that I won't anticipate all their questions. And I'm afraid I won't accurately represent my knowledge of the material or my commitment to the success of the project.	

BUSINESS CASE #2	YOUR NEXT GREAT QUESTION
CLIENT: I have a huge opportunity by taking on this new role, but it is a big risk. **COACH:** What is the risk? **CLIENT:** I might fail!	

BUSINESS CASE #3	YOUR NEXT GREAT QUESTION
CLIENT: I'm still unsure of how to structure the organization. **COACH:** What are your concerns? **CLIENT:** I don't want more than ten direct reports and I need to juggle the reporting relationships to lower the number.	

Below is a sample of our suggested possible responses from the coach:

Sample Business Cases

BUSINESS CASE #1	SUGGESTED NEXT GREAT QUESTIONS
CLIENT: I'm nervous. I have my first presentation in front of the management team next month. **COACH:** What are you concerned about? **CLIENT:** I'm most nervous that I won't anticipate all their questions. And I'm afraid I won't accurately represent my knowledge of the material or my commitment to the success of the project.	**COACH:** • Want to do some brainstorming together of the possible questions and your answers? • Would you like to talk about some ideas together? • What specifically can you do to prepare? • What specifically can you do to demonstrate your commitment? • What are your options for how to handle being stumped by a question?

- What's your game plan to prepare?

- What's a good response if you don't know the answer to the question?

- What would make you feel really good and at ease?

- What does it feel like to believe you know the answers based on all your hard work?

BUSINESS CASE #2	SUGGESTED NEXT GREAT QUESTIONS

COACH:

- Can you say more?

- What issues might lead to failure?

- In what order of importance would you put those issues?

CLIENT: I have a huge opportunity by taking on this new role, but it is a big risk.

- What can you do to address the number one issue?

- What can you do to increase the likelihood of your success?

COACH: What is the risk?

CLIENT: I might fail!

- What if you succeed?

- What do you want?

- What would it look like to succeed?

	• May we explore that some more?
	• How do you suppose it will all work out?
	• What's the action plan?
	• If your life depended on taking some action, what would you do?

BUSINESS CASE #3	SUGGESTED NEXT GREAT QUESTIONS
CLIENT: I'm still unsure of how to structure the organization. **COACH:** What are your concerns? **CLIENT:** I don't want more than ten direct reports and I need to juggle the reporting relationships to lower the number.	**COACH:** • What are your options? • What are other ways you can align the organization? • What is the risk in changing the current structure? • What would it look like ideally? • What feels right in your gut?

3. **Start Coaching.** The purpose of this exercise is to practice your coaching skills. With a willing partner, take about 15 minutes to "coach" on any particular topic of interest. We suggest you choose a real, but not too heavy topic. For example, maybe your partner has a habit they need to work on like keeping their calendar organized. Try your skills out with a manageable problem. This is not the space to solve whether someone should change jobs. For purposes of this exercise, do your best to use

open-ended, vertical, questions that begin with the word "What" as you play the role of the coach. Remember, coaching requires an active collaboration on the part of the coachee and the coach. As the coach, it's your job to ask good questions to help the person being coached come to a decision on their own. When you are done with the coaching session, ask yourself the following questions to debrief:

- Did you use open-ended, vertical questions that began with "What?"

- Did the person being coached feel heard and listened to?

- What characteristics would the person being coached use to describe your coaching style?

- Did you ask permission to share your thoughts, advice, or counsel?

- According to the person being coached, was the coaching conversation useful, productive, and helpful?

- What, if anything, do you need to do more—or less—of next time you coach?

- What was easy for you about coaching? What was hard?

- What was the impact of the coaching?

_____

_____

_____

_____

_____

_____

16

Reviewing Performance

Here's good news. If you do everything we've recommended prior to this chapter, then reviewing an employee's performance will be easy. If you use your listening skills to implement short regular coaching conversations with your team members, the annual review will be a slam-dunk. It's simply a natural extension of those conversations, only a tad more formal.

We recognize that many organizations conduct an annual or semi-annual appraisal process. We won't debate the pros and cons of this practice. We must, however, mention that waiting until the yearly review to advise an employee of poor performance is unthinkable. The same is true for good performance, for that matter. Put yourself in their position. Imagine successfully completing a project but getting no feedback from your boss until months afterward.

A Story from Jon

When I was starting out, I experienced two bosses over the course of two years.

177

The first boss gave me hardly any feedback unless it gave him a chance to be sarcastic. The days leading up to my annual review were full of anxiety. In the review session he would give me a number of favorable comments. However, any positive comment was usually diminished by the conjunction "but," followed by some veiled criticism.

In the course of that year, the only mention of my personal development was made during this review. It consisted of a list of things I could be better at but neglected to project where I might be able to go in the organization.

Frankly, I felt the review was a rationalization for where he'd pegged me in the merit pool. This formal documentation was meant to discourage me from challenging any award I thought too small.

My next boss was the polar opposite. He was always making his expectations clear and continually giving me feedback... more often positive, but negative when necessary. Frequently he asked me about my aspirations and helped me understand how to prepare for the future.

This was the first executive to ask me to write my own annual review. That may be a common practice now, but back then it was unheard of.

Well, it was the best review experience I'd ever had! As I articulated my accomplishments, my boss would echo or expand upon them. This was his way of encouraging me to repeat those behaviors.

When I did my best to polish up an error made during the previous year, this boss would ask if we could talk about that situation. Our dialog would become a means to further coach me and strengthen my performance in the future. In retrospect, I now know that he picked the areas to coach very carefully. His intention was to encourage me—not discourage me.

Unlike my previous boss, this boss asked me open-ended questions. He wanted to know if the support I was getting was sufficient. And he was interested in what I could see myself doing in the future. For that, I think I was most grateful. He wasn't afraid of any answers he might get to these questions. He knew that they existed whether they were out in the open or not.

Was he afraid that by pumping me up I'd think that I was worth more than they were paying? Apparently not. He was prepared to defend his decisions on my compensation if necessary. But the thought of challenging him after such a productive meeting was far from my mind.

KEY THOUGHT

The annual review should be a summation of all the performance conversations you have had during that review period. It should also include opportunities for your direct reports to discuss career aspirations and provide you with candid feedback.

Why did gathering Jon's input in advance of his review enhance the process? It's probably due to that element of control that we mentioned in previous chapters. If one has some measure of control over what is being discussed, they will have more commitment to the conversation. Does this method work for most employees?

With a top performer (*like Jon* ☺), yes.

With an average performer, the leader will have to make careful decisions about when to intervene. You don't want to contradict the other person necessarily; you want to provoke them with open-ended questions that will lead them to think more clearly.

When the leader feels it is important to share their opinion, they should use the techniques we share in Chapter 8. That includes asking for permission to share those ideas.

With poor performers, you'll need to lay the groundwork for a more direct conversation long before review day. You, your boss, and HR should be aligned about the message that will be articulated. And if you have been doing your job throughout the year, this won't come as a surprise to the employee.

There are some additional benefits of gathering the employee's input before their review. For one, it's a great way to determine if you both are in alignment about the employee's performance. If you agree with everything that they plan to share in the review process, then you've just eliminated any potential anxiety. The meeting is bound to be shorter yet deeper. And it will be more focused on the future...where it should be!

Imagine on the other hand, that there is a huge disconnect between what you perceive and what they share with you in advance of your meeting. What went wrong? What role did you play in this misunderstanding? What have they misconstrued? At least now you have a heads up and can prepare some great questions for them...and for yourself.

SKILL-BUILDING EXERCISES

1. **Prepare for the Review.** The goal of this exercise is to help you prepare a solid list of coaching questions geared toward a performance review conversation. Take time to review the examples below and then generate at least five more good questions that you could ask.

   Examples

   - *What are you most proud of accomplishing this year?*
   - *What has gone well since we last talked?*
   - *What could have gone better?*
   - *What made the difference in achieving this goal?*
   - *You may be right that the results were impacted by (the economy, a coworker, another department). What part did you have control over? What could you have done differently?*
   - *What can be done in the future?*
   - *What support do you need from me?*

   Now create a list of at least five more questions.

   _____

   _____

   _____

   _____

   _____

   _____

_____

_____

_____

_____

_____

_____

2. **Individual Development.** Focusing on the individual development and aspirations of your direct reports should be a natural extension of reviewing performance and planning for the coming year. The goal of this exercise is to help you generate some conversation starters to better engage in this type of conversation. Take a look at the examples below.

Examples

- *What do you see yourself doing in the future?*

- *What skills or experiences are required to be successful?*

- *What challenges are you likely to meet along the way?*

- *What one thing could you start this year that would help you along that path?*

- *What can I do to hold you accountable for that action?*

- *What support do you need from me?*

- *What assignments, experiences, exposure, or opportunities do we need to consider in order to support your career aspirations?*

Now, it's your turn. Take a moment to think of five more questions you could ask one of your direct reports as you put together an individual development plan.

_____

_____

_____

_____

_____

_____

_____

_____

_____

_____

3. **Practice Sharing Your Feedback.** Your employees are counting on hearing your opinion and thoughts about their performance. The goal of this exercise is to practice asking permission to give your feedback and think about good questions to help you do just that. Take a look at some examples below:

- *I agree that those things have gone well. May I share some of my thoughts (or concerns) with you?*

- *I see that you took action when things did not go well. May I share some ideas of other actions you could consider next time?*

- *The career path you desire sounds interesting. May we talk about some of the barriers you may confront along the way?*

Now, take the time to craft a few more questions to gain permission to share your thoughts.

_____

_____

_____

_____

_____

_____

_____

_____

_____

_____

_____

_____

_____

_____

_____

_____

17

Decision Making

We were asked by the CEO of a financial services company to lead his management team through a leadership development process. Our program included a kickoff meeting, 360-feedback for each participant, and a closing meeting where we would share the common themes that we discovered during the feedback sessions. The closing meeting would help determine the topics for the leadership development training and coaching that would follow.

The CEO was clearly a talented individual who had rapidly expanded the firm's business. He prided himself on establishing a winning culture in the organization and he appeared to be admired by his staff.

After the kickoff meeting, the HR executive mentioned that we would have to do our best to shorten the closing meeting. We indicated that we needed at least two hours to cover the content. She said the CEO was impatient with the pace of the kickoff meeting and would like the closing meeting to take no more than 60 minutes.

We were puzzled, until we saw the results of the 360-degree surveys. Many of the senior leaders scored abnormally high in showing loyalty to the organization by "respecting the opinions of those in authority." From this result we speculated that the senior leaders were too often deferring to the CEO.

And we were right! In the closing meeting, we saw this behavior in action. The group discussed a subject for a few minutes which was immediately followed by the CEO announcing his decision. Apparently, this was the CEO's definition of collaboration.

Okay, so yes, he had a great batting average when it came to making the right business decisions. But what did he lose by rapidly moving ahead without truly listening?

- **He might have overlooked an option that was better than his own.**

- **He possibly reduced the commitment his team will have for the decision.**

- **He reduced the developmental potential of the situation. When we hear how someone thinks, we may be able to identify an opportunity to harness their strengths or assist them in learning something new.**

- **He ignored an opportunity to foster teamwork. When you witness how others interact, you can determine how independently the group can operate without your presence.**

KEY THOUGHT

The strategy of encouraging participation in decision making is worth considering. It increases confidence in the decision, raises commitment for the execution, and develops the individual and the team all at once.

At this point in the book, it should be no surprise to you that we think great questions can play a major role in good decision making. When you insert great questions into any process, you'll magnify your success.

A formal decision-making process will likely take more time at first, but mix together a couple of great questions with a little bit of structure and a lot of practice and the pace of group decision-making will pick up in a jiffy!

Even if you already have a process for driving decisions, you may find it useful to steal some ideas from our version. The effective use of the questions we list will help you avoid those long, often rambling discussions where most of the decisions are made in the last five minutes of the meeting.

Decision-Making Process

1.   What **specifically** needs to be decided?

2.   What is our **authority** in making this decision?

3.   What will a **good decision** look like?

4.   What is our **readiness** to make a decision?

5.   What **alternatives** do we have?

6.   What is the **best** option?

7.   What does our **plan** look like?

The best way to understand how these seven questions drive the process is to see it in action. So, let's take a look at a real-life situation.

A story from Jon

A few months after I took on a new assignment, a critical problem surfaced. I was in the process of assimilating an acquisition into a $2 billion corporation when I was alerted by the Food and Drug Administration that one of our products was unsafe. There were numerous urgent decisions to be made. As the new executive on the ground, I had a significant responsibility without a great deal of foreknowledge. There was no way that I was going to solve this on my own.

For the sake of demonstrating the collaborative decision-making process we've described in this chapter, I'll share with you how we identified and fixed one of the issues that needed to be resolved.

The product in question was a piece of medical equipment comprised of molded plastic components used in a critical care environment.

Decision Process

QUESTIONS	ANSWERS
What **specifically** needs to be decided? • Are there several decisions to be made? • If so, in what order should they be made?	There were many dependent elements. Our top priorities were: • What is the seriousness of the failure? • What should we do about existing product? • What resources are needed to identify the root cause of the product failures?

QUESTIONS	ANSWERS
What is our **authority** in making this decision? • Can we decide for ourselves or just influence others?	For the most part we had the authority to act while keeping our corporate parent informed. We would need to seek approval if spending would exceed our delegated authority.
What will a **good decision** look like? • Brainstorm (without debate) a list of outcomes the group wants. • Clarify everyone's understanding of the contents of the list. • Discuss. See where there is a consensus. • If necessary, probe those areas where there are differences.	We brainstormed the list of desired outcomes and there was a great deal of consensus in the room. The group quickly identified the highest priority—the need to stop product failures in the field. Steps were taken to alert users to the potential for failure. After the meeting we word-smithed the rest of our desired outcomes: • Stop failures in the field immediately. • Determine the reasons for the failures. Make changes that assure we can provide a defect-free and reliable product going forward.

QUESTIONS	ANSWERS
What is our **readiness** to make a decision? • What more information do we need before we can decide?	We definitely needed more information. We created 3 teams to: • Gather information on what was failing. • Search our data for patterns of failure. • See if we could replicate failures. Our findings were used to create what is called a "fishbone" diagram, an excellent tool for organizing potential root causes. It took 3 months to determine that there was a flaw in the original design. We also determined that a newly manufactured item would not fail until it was used repeatedly.
What **alternatives** do we have? • Brainstorm a list of options. List every input. Do not debate these items.	We broadened the size of our team to include a wider range of expertise. We brainstormed without restraint. Even the experts weren't allowed to cause "brain-stopping".
What is the **best** option? • **For each option**, evaluate the probability of it satisfying your criteria for a **good decision.**	The list of alternatives was long! Three options rose to the top: • For immediate pain relief, supply customers with newly manufactured parts of the old design. • Meanwhile, build new tooling to produce reliable parts. • Finally, replace everything in the field with new reliable parts when available.

QUESTIONS	ANSWERS
What does our **plan** look like?	I maintained overall responsibility for the project.
• What responsibilities are assumed for implementation of the decision?	Elements of the action plan were delegated to key resources who had led the 3 initial decision-making teams.

Okay, we admit that the first time you try to navigate your way through a process like this, it may feel like a lot of work. However, each time you repeat the process, you'll all understand it better until eventually, it becomes transparent.

This process can help you turn a non-productive free-form discussion into a forum for asking really great questions, the answers to which become the underpinning of even better decisions. They will be better because a good process with great questions will expose the underlying differences that group members have when valuing possible alternatives. Left undetected, these differences could become a silent impediment to agreement, commitment, and action.

Take a look at the exercises starting on the next page and see if you can harness the decision-making power of others by asking questions.

SKILL-BUILDING EXERCISES

1. **Decision-Making Process.** The goal of this exercise is to support you in asking more great questions by getting comfortable with a decision-making process. Focus on the *questions* that will support you in reaching the best decision.

Use this chart to help you tackle a decision you need to make:

DECISION-MAKING PROCESS	GREAT QUESTIONS TO ASK	NOTES FOR YOUR CONVERSATION
What **specifically** needs to be decided?		
What is your **authority** in making this decision?		
What will a **good decision** look like?		
What is your **readiness** to make the best choice?		
What is the **best** option?		
What does your **plan** look like?		

2. **Great Decisions.** Think about some recent decisions you have made—both good and bad. To help you better sort your list, assume "good" decisions generally share a few common characteristics:

    a. The decision sticks

    b. Both you and your team were committed to the decision

    c. You reached a successful outcome

Think about the process you undertook to make the decision. Now make a list of what worked well for the good decisions and what didn't work well for the bad decisions.

For example:

WHAT I DID TO CREATE A "GOOD" DECISION	WHAT I DID TO CREATE A "POOR" DECISION
• Gathered ideas from coworkers and team regarding decision	• Didn't ask others for their thoughts about the decision
• Asked more questions!!!	• Missed an opportunity for harnessing teamwork to generate greater commitment for a decision
• Allowed team to feel mutual ownership of the decision process	
• Brainstormed a complete list of options	• Assumed I had more influence in a decision-making process than I really did
• Gained a valuable perspective into how others think	
• Determined our readiness to make a decision	• Didn't consider all the options
• Determined our options	• Talked too much and didn't listen enough to others
• Made a good plan to execute the decision	• Already made up my mind before I involved others

Use the following space to create your own list:

Decision: _____

_____

_____

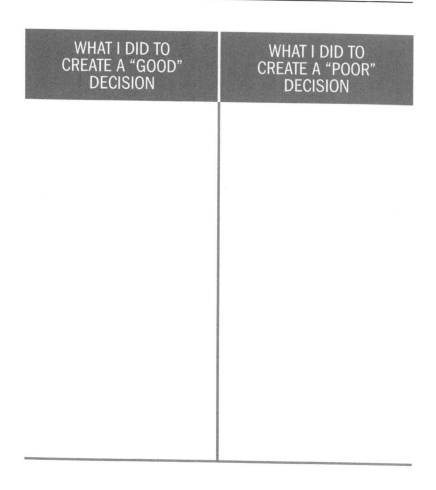

WHAT I DID TO CREATE A "GOOD" DECISION	WHAT I DID TO CREATE A "POOR" DECISION

Now, reflect on what you wrote above and apply it to an upcoming decision. Given what you've learned, what do you need to focus on to create consistently "good" decisions in the future?

3. **Pocket List of Questions.** The goal of this exercise is to help you consider some of the questions you may want to ask regarding an upcoming decision. First think about a decision you are currently grappling with. Then identify a person you need to involve in the decision. Finally, brainstorm a list of important questions to help you navigate the conversation. Refer to the example below.

Decision: *The scope of our redesigning a technical program application.*

Person I should consult with: *Lucy*

DECISION-MAKING PROCESS QUESTIONS	MY QUESTIONS
What **specifically** needs to be decided?	What do we want to take on in this redesign project? What would the scope be?
What is our **authority** in making this decision?	What involvement do we need outside our organization? Who is impacted by this application? What does it look like to make decisions together on this redesign project? What involvement do you want to have in making decisions throughout the process? At what point do you want to be consulted or informed?

DECISION-MAKING PROCESS QUESTIONS	MY QUESTIONS
What will a **good decision** look like?	What is our end product? What are the top user criteria? What is the look and feel we want? What are the most important elements to you in this redesign project?
What is our **readiness** to make a decision?	What other information do we need? What is our budget and timing?
What **alternatives** do we have?	What things do you want to be sure we consider in this process? What different approaches to the redesign could we take? What do similar applications look like? What are your thoughts about hiring another programmer?
What is the **best** option?	What do you think the best options are? We've discussed many options. May I summarize what I think we agree upon?
What does our **plan** look like?	What is your understanding of what we plan to do?

Create your own pocket list in the next column. Think of an upcoming decision and the person with whom you should consult.

DECISION-MAKING PROCESS QUESTIONS	MY QUESTIONS
What **specifically** needs to be decided?	
What is our **authority** in making this decision?	
What will a **good decision** look like?	
What is our **readiness** to make a decision?	
What **alternatives** do we have?	
What is the **best** option?	
What does our **plan** look like?	

4. **A Good Example.** This exercise will help you reflect on how it feels to be a part of a successful decision-making process. Think about a recent "successful" decision you were a part of, but did not lead. Reflect on the actions the leader exhibited to help create the positive outcome. Jot down a few of your ideas.

_____

_____

_____

_____

_____

What did you learn from this experience?

_____

_____

_____

What is the one action or change that would make the most difference in your decision-making?

_____

_____

_____

_____

18

Leading Change

A client wanted our participation in their announcement to employees about a major corporate change initiative. Here was their plan as they presented it to us: The CEO would give a short PowerPoint presentation about the strategy. Then each senior market leader would spend 30 minutes explaining why this would be good for the business. Then, they proposed, we would speak for 30 minutes, helping employees understand their role in *accepting* the change.

We were reluctant to take the assignment if that was the way things would go. Their entire presentation was designed to *persuade* employees that this change was a good thing, and the only impediment to its success was **their** resistance.

In the midst of change, people yearn to be listened to— NOT persuaded.

What are the main reasons for employing listening so diligently in the midst of change?

- **It shows respect for those impacted by the change**
- **The interaction helps you measure acceptance of the change**
- **Asking questions surfaces barriers to the change**
- **Repeated interaction gradually moves the focus from the past to the future**

More than fifty percent of major change initiatives fail to meet their ultimate goals, due in part to a common misunderstanding of what it takes to overcome the natural resistance to change. Leaders must become change agents. They need to understand the psychology of change—denial, resistance, exploration and commitment—and use communication skills that accelerate everyone through this natural process.

Here's a Story from Jon

Back in Chapter 3, I shared that I was tasked with the combining of two businesses, which meant closing several locations. I knew this would be earth-shattering for many employees. I gave careful thought about how I could communicate the news.

Standing in front of the employee population, I made this brief announcement: "The decision has been made to close this facility. This is not at all a reflection of your performance. The facility will close 12 months from now. Only a handful of employees will be offered relocation to the new facility. In the next few days you will get detailed information on how this impacts each of you and the ways in which we can support you in transitioning to new employment. We'll meet again soon to answer any questions you may have."

There was clearly shock in the room. A few people were crying. Nobody had the capacity to absorb any persuasive PowerPoint presentations. Their thoughts were appropriately selfish: "Why did I just buy that new house?;" "How am I going to make my car payments?;" "I haven't looked for a job in 15 years."

Initially, in bad news announcements like this, bare facts are the most you should provide. Be honest and direct. It's a good idea to develop a list of talking points in anticipation of every question they might have. But frankly, your audience will not be capable of processing any answer you supply, even if they can articulate the question.

When you meet soon after (several hours or a day), you'll need to really listen to your employees. By asking open-ended, vertical questions that begin with "What", you will come to learn what they want to know.

Next, plan to have a one-on-one conversation with every key employee. These are your high performers, potential successors, and those who possess critical knowledge, skills, or relationships.

Here are some questions you might want to ask:

1. **What are your thoughts about the changes we announced?**

2. **It sounds like you have several concerns. What is the most important one?**

3. **What are your thoughts about how we can resolve that concern?**

4. **What impact do these changes have on you?**

5. **What barriers stand in the way of this being successful?**

6. **What do we need to do to overcome those barriers?**

You may wonder how long the "wake" of the announcement will last. Well, that depends on the severity of the change as perceived by those who are impacted. You are not the judge—they are. In the meantime, you should expect to continue having conversations with your key people until you feel a majority of them have begun to accept the "future state." When they begin thinking about what to do next—instead of what piece of the past they have lost—you'll know they are on the verge of acceptance.

As a rule, it'll take longer than you'd like. But if you rush the process, it will force concerns underground and you'll find that the long-term impact on productivity is profound.

A Positive Step to Take

You can accelerate acceptance by providing a process for identifying barriers to the change. Choose an Issues Clarification Process that can be used both one-on-one and with groups.

You can find a sample of the Issues Clarification Process we use on our website: **www.WhatYouDontKnowAboutListening.com**

We have used this process hundreds of times with demonstrated success. The mere act of listing some barriers helps some participants put those concerns in perspective. This organized listening activity will zero in on problems that can be addressed, while encouraging forward-thinking initiatives. Overcoming an identified barrier gives a sense of achievement that is powerful in moving people through change.

There is one caution. Leaders who use this process—but then don't act upon the input given—will risk hardening the employees' resistance. Why? Because this demonstrates that they weren't really listening!

Change is rarely easy or simple. Using your listening skills and asking good questions will help you better navigate change and turn the tide from denial and negativity to exploration and commitment.

Below are some exercises to help you explore your own style when dealing with change. They will help you practice listening and asking good questions during change initiatives.

SKILL-BUILDING EXERCISES

1. **Awareness Check.** Some people embrace change and dive headfirst into the new. Others immediately resist and dig their heels in, stubborn and unwilling to budge. Others get angry, or sad, or may be stunned by the shock. Whatever your gut reaction, it's important to understand your own personal inclinations so that you are aware of how you perceive and react to change. We often think others will react or behave as we do... but when it comes to change (and life in general), this isn't true. Answer these questions for yourself:

   - Do you respond to changes emotionally, analytically, or a combination of both?

   - Think about a big change you recently experienced at work or personally. What was your first reaction?

   - What about how you react to change impacts how you lead others through change?

   - How quickly do you cycle through the stages of change? Think of a recent change. Where are you now—in denial, resistance, exploration or commitment?

_____

_____

_____

_____

_____

_____

_____

_____

2. **Emotional Rollercoaster.** Think about a conversation you need to have with someone whose role in the company is changing. Assume they have not yet accepted this. Put together a short list of good questions.

   Examples:

   - What do you think about the recent change?
   - What are you feeling?
   - What issues do we need to consider?
   - What concerns do you have?

   _____

   _____

   _____

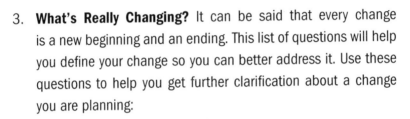

3. **What's Really Changing?** It can be said that every change is a new beginning and an ending. This list of questions will help you define your change so you can better address it. Use these questions to help you get further clarification about a change you are planning:

- What is the actual change—describe it in as much detail as possible. For example, "lower costs" doesn't give much detail. What is actually going to be different?

- What are the impact points of this change? In other words, what are the secondary changes this change will cause?

- What will be lost as a result of the change? What can you do to acknowledge that loss?

- What can you do to give back and balance what is being taken away?

- What is ending? What is staying the same?

- What actions can you take to help people navigate through denial, resistance, and exploration in order to arrive at commitment?

_____

_____

_____

_____

_____

_____

_____

_____

_____

_____

_____

_____

_____

_____

_____

_____

_____

19

Overcoming Conflict

Conflict will always be present in the workplace—it's a natural byproduct of gathering together different people with diverse interests and goals.

Depending on how you react, conflict can either damage or strengthen a relationship. If handled well, it can lead to better outcomes, like increased self-awareness, clearer understanding amongst colleagues, and better decision making. Handled poorly, conflict can do great harm.

There may not be a more important time for you to listen than during the moments when people are in conflict. In this chapter we'll discuss what you can do when you are in the midst of conflict. Once you master these skills, you (in your leadership role), will be able to model these behaviors to your subordinates and intercede when you need to resolve conflict among others.

Barriers to Listening During Conflict

The drive to *win* an argument can be so strong that it prevents someone from listening to their "opponent". So eager to present their own point of view, they'll interrupt to take command of the conversation. They are convinced that their logic will win the day.

Equally strong for some people is the desire to *avoid* an argument. They'll walk away from a situation the moment they are uncomfortable, already convinced that it can't be resolved. They're unable to listen because *they aren't there.*

Either behavior can produce hostility because both parties feel that they are unheard or misunderstood. These feelings can naturally lead to the self-preservation behavior of defensiveness.

When participants are in a defensive mode, progress is unlikely. The first step is to move from defensiveness to behaviors that help resolve the situation.

There are dozens of books on how to resolve conflict. We won't make this chapter a compendium of them all. Instead, we'll focus on the one unique approach that raises your game to a higher level. Will it work 100% of the time? Nothing does. But is there a good chance it will de-escalate the fight? We say yes.

The Secret Sauce of our Approach

- **Pause**

- **Accept responsibility for your role in the conflict (stick with us for a minute on this one)**

- **Ask for help in rectifying the situation**

Here's a Story from Jon

I began my career teaching communications in a high school. Keeping control of the classroom is an early leadership challenge for a first-year teacher. Every student-provoked distraction seems like a challenge to your authority.

One student in particular was getting under my skin. When I would look Mike's way he was talking to the person next to him or just not paying attention. It was also my perception that he arrived late for class nearly every day.

Week after week, I chose not to address the issue until one day when he arrived ten minutes late to class. In frustration, I demanded he accompany me to the principal's office. We left the classroom of his wide-eyed peers and walked silently down the hall. Mike was the first to speak.

Mike: So, why are we going to the principal's office?

Mr. White: Because I'm tired of you coming late to class.

Mike: But others come late to class and you haven't brought them to the principal's office.

*I stopped dead in my tracks. (**Pause**) I knew that Mike was right. It was clear in this moment that I had a choice. I could hear that truth and allow for it or stand my authoritarian ground and force Mike into detention. (**Accept Responsibility**)*

Mr. White: You're right, I haven't. Let's go back to class.

*Walking back down the hall, we shared the perceptions that led to my outburst of frustration. I asked Mike what we could do to improve the situation. (**Ask for help**) He said that if I had a concern with his behavior, he wanted me to tell him privately and in a timely manner. He also wanted other students to get the same treatment. Fair enough! We had arrived at a commitment to work more openly with one another and Mike was never late for class again.*

I learned a lot about leadership that day.

Let's deconstruct our "Secret Sauce" recipe for resolving conflict. Before reading on, you can review "The 4 W's" in Chapter 7, *Push Pause to Listen.*

Pause

The pause is that brief de-escalation that helps ratchet down the adrenaline and turn on the cooperative, consensual, or even empathetic behaviors needed to resolve the issue.

How do you create a pause? Just admit that you need time to think and collect yourself. You may need a moment to take a deep breath and relax. Or, you might ask the other party if you could recess now and meet again in the next day or two.

If the other person has already become angry, stay calm. Use non-threatening body language and tone of voice. Remember to keep people and problems separate.

Don't use this pause as an opportunity to avoid or escalate the conflict. Use it to study the situation.

KEY THOUGHT
Your ultimate goal during conflict:

- *Avoid being aggressive or submissive during the exchange.*

- *Encourage the other person's participation.*

- *Present a confident and assertive message.*

So, what do you do in the midst of pausing to reach your ultimate goal? Begin by asking yourself this one very important, open-ended question. *What is my role in this conflict?*

Accepting Responsibility

If you are completely honest with yourself, you'll find some way in which you have contributed to a conflicted situation. This is not a court of law. Admitting your role is not a weakness—it's a strength. When you announce your part in the conflict, you disarm the other arguments in the room. Now the other person doesn't feel obligated to be defensive.

Here are some questions to ask yourself. If you don't have the answers, these may be questions you can ask the other person.

- **What have I said?**
  - » If you said something in anger or spite, you may have hardened the other person's resistance.

- **What have I ignored?**
  - » If you were aware of a problem but hoped it would go away, the situation may have become more difficult for the other person.

- **What goals were not clear?**
  - » If you recognize that you delegated a task without confirming understanding, you may be responsible for the failure. (Avoid inferring that the other person is incapable of understanding!)

- **What assumptions did I make without confirming?**
  - » If there's new information that challenges assumptions you made when you assigned the responsibility, you may need to cut them some slack.

- **What expectations did I have that were unrealistic?**
  - » You want to set the bar high, but if you are always pushing the limits, you may be discouraging this person.

- **What resources did I withhold?**
  - » If you ignored requests for help, you may have made the assignment more difficult to accomplish.

- **What rewards did I provide that stood in the way of cooperation?**
  - » In an effort to encourage performance, you may have set up individuals to compete with one another, unwittingly increasing the probability of conflict.

If these questions have not uncovered a role that you played in the conflict, they can provide you with the script of questions to ask while you closely listen. To listen effectively, calmly ask vertical questions that show you are interested in getting the other person's point of view. Your patience will lower defensiveness and build openness. In the end, you will have the opportunity to assert yourself if you discover you are not culpable.

Asking for Help

When you ask someone to express their ideas first, you signal a willingness to listen to them. Some examples:

- **What do you think we should do to solve this issue?**
- **What do we need to do to move forward?**
- **What stands in the way of our getting this done?**

If this approach is new to them, they may be reluctant to contribute. Be patient. Make the request again calmly, using slightly different words. For example:

- **What have you seen others do to overcome a situation like this?**

- **What has worked for you in the past?**

You can always weigh in once you get them contributing. Hone the skills needed to share your opinion by referring to Chapter 8, *Offering Your Opinion.*

It takes courage to do this. Courage to listen and to assure someone that they have been heard. Hearing someone doesn't mean that you have to agree with them—you are simply allowing them to articulate their perception of the situation. Don't fear that your behavior will be perceived as weakness. Your courage is bound to be admired and it reflects your strength as a leader.

Try your hand at some of the exercises below to support your ability to use listening skills in conflict situations.

SKILL-BUILDING EXERCISES

1. **What is Your Natural Reaction to Conflict?** Understanding your natural reaction will help you better understand why you need to **pause** to more effectively resolve conflict. Once you understand your tendencies, you can use good questions to improve your listening skills. So, think about what you naturally do when it comes to conflict:

    a. Are you naturally more competitive and feel a strong desire to win OR do you take a more relaxed approach and prefer to back off in the heat of competition?

b. Are you naturally more aggressive in conflict OR do you become more passive and prefer avoidance?

c. Do you naturally begin to talk louder, more quickly, and more intensely OR do you get quiet, pull back, and become more reserved?

2. **Push Pause. What is Really Important Here?** Before you have that conversation, use these questions to help you reflect on what you really want to accomplish.

QUESTION	NOTES
What is my real purpose?	
What impact will my trying to win have on the situation? OR What impact will my trying to avoid the conflict have on the situation?	
What is critical to me about this issue?	
What is critical to the other person?	

QUESTION	NOTES
What impact will an escalation of conflict have on our future relationship?	

3. **Explore Options Together.** One of the most powerful parts of asking good questions in a conflicted situation is that it helps you to preserve the relationship and move forward collaboratively. Think about a situation in which you are experiencing conflict. List a series of open-ended, vertical, "What" questions to help you move the conversation forward.

   My conflict situation:

   _____

   _____

   My questions to help move the conversation forward:

   _____

   _____

   _____

   _____

   _____

   _____

Afterword: What You NOW Know About Listening

In our coaching practice, we've been fortunate to have the opportunity to help so many leaders improve their communication skills. In doing so, we were able to isolate the specific behaviors that changed the way people were listening to one another. That is why we have been so excited to share our powerful concepts with you.

Rather than confound you with a thousand ways you might change, our approach has been to take a deep dive into the singular ability to ask great questions. Improvement comes more easily to our "students" when we focus on the few (not the many) tenets of good listening.

So, in summary, we advocate that you...

Ask More...

Open-ended questions to show people that you are really interested in what they have to say. This behavior will enhance the perception that you are truly concerned about them, value them, and want to be supportive.

Ask More…

Vertical questions to show that you are really curious about the point-of-view of others. This behavior will demonstrate that, even when you disagree with someone, you are willing to hear their ideas. It also increases their willingness to hear what you have to say.

Ask More…

Questions that **begin with the word "What"** to reduce defensiveness. Though no single word can eliminate the existence of feelings that may have built up over time, using "what" questions helps to put the other person at ease. You'll find that the content and outcome of your conversations will significantly improve.

The Most Valuable Reward

Once you've mastered this remarkable skill, you might discover that listening has become your greatest strength.

"…a growing body of research suggests that the way to influence— and to lead—is to begin with warmth. Warmth is the conduit of influence; it facilitates trust and the communication and absorption of ideas.

*Prioritizing warmth helps you connect immediately with those around you, demonstrating that you **hear** them, understand them, and can be trusted by them."*[1]

---

1 Cuddy, Kohut, and Neffinger, Harvard Business Review, (July-August 2013)

Listening is the one leadership behavior that most conveys warmth.

Your Legacy

Now it's time for us to ask YOU a question. What do you want your legacy to be?

We hope that someday, when you reflect on your leadership career, you'll see a past defined by success. Your memories will include the times you thought strategically about the company's future and drew followers to that vision with a style of communication that excited them and created loyalty.

If anything we have shared in **What You Don't Know About Listening** supports that legacy, we would be most pleased!

Thanks for listening,

Jon and Alexandra

We would enjoy hearing from you. Contact us at:

www.WhatYouDontKnowAboutListening.com

MEET THE AUTHORS

Jon F. White

Jon White began his career as an educator; not surprisingly, his subject was Communications. He moved on to build a small chain of travel agencies which later sold for ten times the initial investment. Following that, Jon spent 20 years as a successful top-level business leader in the medical device industry.

Mr. White now infuses his work as an Executive Coach, Leadership Consultant, and valued Speaker with the practical knowledge he brought from each of his past experiences.

Jon has worked with senior leaders throughout North America, Europe, the Middle East and Asia and has consulted for a wide range of companies, including: QualComm, Jenny Craig, Disney, Black and Decker, Callaway Golf, Chrysler, Kinder Morgan, Ingram Micro, Fieldstone Communities, Quest Diagnostics, and State Street Financial, to name just a few.

With a passionate interest in the behaviors necessary to provide outstanding leadership, Jon's professional journey has led him to focus on Listening because he believes it to be the skill that is fundamental to almost all other leadership attributes.

Alexandra Barton Taketa

Alexandra Taketa is a certified executive coach and an experienced Learning and Development professional. She thrives on working with leaders to build the skills necessary for success. Alexandra has coached executives of Fortune 500 companies, non-profits and governmental organizations including: Gap Inc., Allergan, Motorola, AdFlight, Hewlett Packard, Environmental Protection Agency, and Amigos de las Americas. She has held senior Learning and Talent Development roles at Allergan, Gap Inc., and Mercer Management Consulting.

Alexandra is expert at creating leadership and management development programs, developing competency models, orchestrating succession planning, and facilitating cross-functional and enterprise-wide organization design initiatives.

A proud mother of two, Alexandra is an old soul, a natural teacher, and a masterful listener who brings a rich and dynamic spirit and energy to her work.

Made in the USA
San Bernardino, CA
04 May 2015